KEEPING THE PROMISE

A WORK ETHIC FOR DOING THINGS RIGHT

LARRY KENNEDY, PH.D.

Reliable Man® Books
Email: Admin@LarryKennedy.com
http://www.LarryKennedy.com

Keeping the Promise™
Business and Continuing Education Seminars
Contact Creative Management Services, Inc.
Email: Seminars@LarryKennedy.com
http://www.LarryKennedy.com

Definitions are from the *Merriam-Webster Dictionary*

To protect the privacy of individuals and families, I have changed the names of some persons and places, as well as other details not significant to the lesson. It is my desire to convey the important facts and principles necessary for vocational growth without bringing harm to any person.

I am blessed to have found a faithful partner in life who shares my passion for doing things right. My precious wife, Dorothy, has always kept her promises. She has been a shining example of reliable ethics and vocational excellence.

TABLE OF CONTENTS

Author's Preface

America is experiencing an ethical crisis. If today's shopping list requires anything more than taking a familiar product off of a well-known supplier's shelf, you will be challenged by the ethical crisis in America. If you have your car repaired or speak to a craftsman about installing or remodeling something in your home or office, you will be challenged by the ethical crisis in America. If you sit in a classroom, either to teach or be taught, you will be challenged by the ethical crisis in America. If you discuss your health or well-being with a care-giver, lawyer, or insurance company, you will be challenged by the ethical crisis in America. If you call a government agency, read a newspaper, listen to the radio, watch television, or attend a sports or entertainment event, you will be challenged by the ethical crisis in America. Or, if you are a manager or professional who must try to fulfill your promises to your customers through an employee's efforts, you will be challenged by the ethical crisis in America.

The Merriam-Webster dictionary defines "ethics" as the discipline dealing with what is good and bad, and with moral duty and obligation. An "ethic" is a system or guiding philosophy of moral values and principles of conduct. When people share the same ethic, they can buy and sell, have reasonable conversations and generally depend upon one another to do things right and keep their promises. Ethics strengthen our conscience, restrain us from selfish or unfair acts, or help us empathize with another person's problem so we can do the right thing to help them. An ethic must be taught and modeled by all parts of a community for it to remain vital. When we fail to teach ethics at home, at school, and at work, we lose our ability to have reasonable conversations and function reliably in the marketplace.

When I was a boy, I was taught to "treat others the way you want them to treat you." It was called the "Golden Rule" and it was something I heard at home, at school, on the ball field, and virtually anywhere people wanted to work or play together in a friendly, orderly manner. Although the Golden Rule was not followed by everyone, the majority of the people we came into contact with each

9

day were aware that their actions would be judged by that simple standard. So when business leaders like W. Edwards Deming and Philip Crosby trained their clients to manage people and processes, they were building upon a generally-accepted foundation of ethics. However, by the end of their careers, they had to adjust to a deteriorating work ethic and emphasize the ethical "ingredients" required for their philosophy of management to succeed. Without a renewal of ethical standards, people could no longer be relied upon to embrace the honesty and accountability required to function effectively at work.

If you are disturbed by the deterioration of ethical standards in America, and are already doing things right at home and at work, we hope you will be encouraged by what you read. But if you are interested in new ways to discuss the effects of America's ethical crisis with your staff or co-workers and renew their passion for *doing things right*, we hope *Keeping the Promise* will become part of your plan. It is based upon the premise that all transactions between people are defined by a promise to exchange value for value. To be successful, we must embrace the importance of our promise with a renewed attitude, establish reliable processes, encourage vocational excellence, and expect personal reliability from each member of our team. Like those who have gone before us in every generation, our goal must be to renew the values and principles for *Keeping the Promise.*

Larry Kennedy

KEEPING THE PROMISE

CHAPTER 1
EMBRACE THE PROMISE

☛ Promise

From the beginning of time, the basic transaction between people
has been defined by their promise to exchange value for value with
one another. Since then, the only things that have changed are the
technologies we have developed to help us fulfill our promises.

Imagine an ancient cave-dweller relaxing on his front porch after a long day hunting for food. Across the river at his neighbor's cave, he can hear an almost-constant, clink, clink, clink as the would-be "entrepreneur" pounds away at a piece of rock trying to shape it into something useful. To the hunter, it is an amusing sight as time after time the rock suddenly shatters into a useless heap of stones. But the emerging craftsman is undeterred, eventually developing tools and techniques that allow him to shape the worthless stone into a fully functioning *wheel*. In a short time, he has fashioned the wheel and some tree limbs into a pull-cart allowing him to bring home the bounty from a long hunt with relative ease.

The hunter's amusement turned to envy as he realized the "genius" of his neighbor's efforts. But then he had an idea. If he could persuade the stone-cutter to make another wheel, he could trade for it and build his own cart, enabling him to carry more game. So the hunter and his wife wade across the river with high hopes that the stone-cutter will accept their promise of a hot meal every evening for a month in exchange for their own wheel. This basic transaction, *the promise* to exchange value for value, is the foundation for all business and personal relationships, and the cornerstone of commerce. Since the beginning of time, the only things that have changed are the technologies we have developed to help us fulfill our promises.

The invention of money, cash registers, credit cards, computers, and educational technologies such as Quality Management are the result of competition to discover more effective methods for *keeping the promise*. As each generation of business leaders emerges, we have also learned new and better ways to teach, train, coach, mentor and manage ourselves and others, all for the purpose of *keeping the promise*. We have developed our business efforts into a science, defining how to correctly identify the needs of our customer and then fulfilling his or her requirements. We have also recognized that our customer can be anyone to whom we have made a promise; whether it be a business or personal relationship and/or for profit, for pleasure, or for the common good.

Everyone Has a Story

Sadly, almost everyone I know has a story or stories about supposedly reliable people and companies who have failed to keep their promise. Have you tried to change or update your cell phone or cable service lately? The maze of confusing information and responses can be bewildering. And, all too often, I've had the feeling that the person on the phone or across the counter was "bluffing" their way through the conversation, just like they have seen countless other business and political leaders or poker-players do on television. Their sole objective appeared to be self-serving; to make a sale, or somehow be credited for their contact with me, while getting me off of their computer screen or out the door as soon as possible. And, far too many times, their "help" either confused the issue or sent me hurtling toward an unproductive dead-end. Like most people, I have learned to hang up and call back to, hopefully, get another person who might know the right thing to do. Eventually, I will find a reasonable person who is clearly concerned about keeping the promise; you know, the one who is apologetic about our bad experiences, clear and deliberate in their responses, specifically helpful, *and*, when our contact with them is complete, the promise is kept.

Beyond the wildly ridiculous examples such as Enron, or the many others who have been caught duping their customers or shareholders, the average citizen is now routinely faced with the difficult challenge of deciding whether or not they can rely on the promises that have been given to them.

Late one Friday night, I had just finished installing new telephone and Internet services only to discover that the installation also required me to test the alarm system which protected my home. When I called the alarm company, the first "helper" gave me the wrong test code. Three or four calls later, after I had completed a series of bungled troubleshooting attempts without success, I finally found someone who discovered the first helper's error. But it was only a matter of minutes until another unknown factor was blocking my security system. The next "helper" kept asking me for my password while answering each question with the preface, "I'm just guessing, but. . . ." After several exasperating minutes, I finally said, "You know, this is a very serious problem I am trying to solve. Is there someone I can talk to who wouldn't be 'just guessing' at the answers?" Within seconds, the helper had transferred me to a tech-support voice mail which promised to call me back on Monday. But I had learned to be unrelenting and just two calls later, I found a real helper who quickly gave me the information I needed, completed the test, and kept the promise, allowing me to sleep securely knowing that my system was working properly.

What Did *You* Promise?

As to the people who fail us, someone once told me that they also have a story and "if you knew and understood their story, it would cause you to have compassion for them." So we can't just go around hating everyone and everything that doesn't work right, run on time, or isn't there when he, she, or it is needed. It's true that we should have a reasonable expectation that the promises people and companies make to us will be kept. Even so, we should be willing to forgive people's individual frailties and work through each situation peacefully so that we don't burn inside with anger, *and*, because of our own bad behavior, fail to find someone who is interested in *keeping the promise*.

One way to gain a balanced perspective on *keeping the promise* is to review the list of promises we have made to others. Remember, *our customer can be anyone to whom we have made a promise; whether it be a business or personal relationship and/or for profit, for pleasure, or for the common good.* For instance, we may have made promises to our spouse, children, family, friends, customers, their families, their referral sources, payers, and even to recipients of our charity that we will … What? Imagine how your customers will feel and how you will be perceived by them if you embrace the promise you made and work hard to fulfill it. Then, imagine how your customers will feel if you fail at *keeping the promise* or are indifferent about their attempts to get you to do things right. You have probably had both good and bad experiences as a customer, so just put yourself in the place of the person who failed in *keeping the promise* and ask yourself this simple question: Is that how I want to be perceived? Now, take the other position and think back to one of the times you erupted at someone's failure in *keeping the promise* and personally attacked them with abusive words or vengeful actions. Then answer these questions: First, is that how you would want to be treated for your failures? And second, how often has your ranting caused someone to do things right?

Most people would agree that something is generally wrong with the way people now feel about keeping their promises. And, even though there are good people who still take their promises seriously, there are a large number who do not. Add to this the unreasonable expectations that some of us still have for what the marketplace should be capable of doing, and you have people who are becoming more and more frustrated with their daily routines. The tension this creates is bad enough when we are talking about the dependability of our telephone or cable services. But what if the situation is really serious? What about the failures by licensed professionals who are supposed to be helping people with more serious personal, emotional, or medical problems? Or when we have promised and failed to help a person overcome an addiction or some other life-controlling problem? Or when we have failed to teach or train people in ways that will allow them to attain knowledge so that they can function with competence and wisdom?

The problems we have getting our car repaired or house painted the way it was promised are only symptomatic of a much bigger problem with huge consequences. Too often, people are trying to accomplish their work without a reliable ethic for doing things right. They have lost their fervor for the work ethic which keeps things functioning the way we know they should. This is especially troubling in the helping professions because it is better not to make a promise, than to make one and not keep it. To find our way back, society must embrace the values and principles for *keeping the promise.*

CHAPTER 2
EMPOWER THE PROMISE

☛ Promise

☛ ZD Attitude

We will strive to keep our promise with a Zero Defects attitude. Although we do not expect perfection from any person or process, we will never accept a standard for quality that allows defective products or services to be delivered to our customers.

Zero Defects is a greatly misunderstood term. A Zero Defects attitude is much more than a concept for eliminating defects in a product or service; it is an attitude of the heart. Similar to the "pride of workmanship," it represents a burning desire to do things right, every time we take action. It is not an attempt to achieve perfection but a clear recognition that every customer is important. Zero Defects is a commitment to make each customer's experience as close to what was promised as possible. Everyone is going to make mistakes, show up late once in awhile, or fail to deliver on a promise the way it was intended. But a Zero Defects heart attitude expresses a desire to lower the number of defects in our performance, and when possible, eliminate them.

I have a favorite fast-food restaurant which serves a hot hamburger just the way I like it. After a long day on the road consulting or teaching, I will sometimes excuse myself from an exhausting dinner meeting and head for the familiar drive-through lane with a simple objective: high-protein comfort food. I want to be alone with my sandwich and maybe watch a few minutes of an old movie or a ball game on television. So it is not unusual to see me strolling through the lobby of my hotel with my briefcase in one hand and my take-out bag in the other. I look forward to that sandwich because I can depend upon it. Almost anywhere I travel, it provides a reliable and reasonably healthy alternative to the evening's dinner options.

The Zero Defects Question

Imagine though, settling in for that comforting taste, pulling back the paper wrapper and taking a large first-bite of that sumptuous delight, only to discover that I had just bitten into a worm embedded in my sandwich. A Zero Defects heart attitude answers the question: How many worms in my sandwich are too many? For the customer, one worm is too many. But, do you think the restaurant manager would be satisfied that only one worm made its way into one hamburger, and that several thousand others that day were worm-free? No, he probably hates the thought of such an event, as almost anyone would. A reliable manager would want to assure me of his concerns, search his processes to discover and eliminate the cause of my bad experience, and thus prevent the possibility of a second episode. That is a Zero Defects heart attitude.

There is a flame burning in the heart of everyone with a Zero Defects attitude. As a manager, I want to do everything I can to nurture and encourage that fire and provide the support that is needed to keep it burning hot and bright. It is really quite easy to see whether or not the fire is in a person's heart because it is also in their eyes and hands, and in the many things they say and do while they work. If a person embraces the promise, they demonstrate an enthusiasm for their work that is noticeable. When the fire of a Zero Defects heart attitude is not there, it is just as noticeable.

Lightning Strikes Again and Again

Florida is the lightning capital of the world, and the "light-show" produced by the summer afternoon and evening thunderstorms can be spectacular. Fortunately, we had never experienced a direct hit on our home or any damage. But on one steamy Saturday afternoon a series of loud thunder claps was accompanied by a loud "ssssnap" that surged through the attic and over my head as I stood in the hallway of our home. My wife said, "What was that?" I knew immediately what had happened. We had experienced our first lightning strike. I quickly surveyed the damage to our appliances while I puzzled about how it happened. We had taken special care to "ground" all of the electrical, telephone, and TV cables so that such an event was very unlikely. The TV cable! Oh no! Just that morning the cable repairman had visited, and he had made a very definite impression that he was someone in whom there was no fire for keeping the promise.

The technician had left the job hurriedly, without testing our TV signal, and we soon discovered that his lazy, unresponsive persona was an indicator of his work ethic. We had already reported the failure of the technician's efforts. He had replaced a defective cable that connected to our home, but the picture was still very poor. Soon after the lightning strike, a cable company supervisor arrived at our door. He was bright-faced, yet sober, and quickly discovered two things. The technician had terribly botched his simple cable-splicing assignment, *and*, he had left the protective ground wire unattached when he left, allowing the lightning to run into our home unobstructed. The supervisor apologized, took responsibility for the error, and assured me that he would have someone back to my home within hours to correct the problem. Ah, someone who wanted to keep the promise.

Several days, and a dozen calls later, we discovered that the friendly and helpful supervisor had gone on vacation and had failed to "tag" our work order "high-priority," as he had promised. Each new service agent to whom we had spoken had assured us that someone would be at our home "very soon." However, what was displayed on the computer screen of the service agents had not been forwarded to the repair department. The supervisor's attempt to give our problem special attention had apparently dead-ended into his vacation plans, and was lost on a tiny slip of paper that was never turned in as promised. I worked my way up through the organization, one call at a time, until a senior manager discovered the discrepancy and personally coordinated the repair crew's rapid dispatch to our home.

The repair crew was fantastic. They replaced all of the melted cables in the attic, inventoried the damaged equipment, and had everything documented and in perfect working order when they left. They were clean, orderly, and professional, so I took advantage of their visit to question them about their colleagues' performances. They were craftsmen who still had fire in their hearts and spent most of their time correcting other people's mistakes. They really cared about how they and their company were perceived and were saddened by the lack of concern for keeping the promise that they saw in the new-hires that were joining the company. A few days after the repair crew had finished, a claims adjuster stopped by to inspect the repairs and arrange to reimburse us for our losses. I showed him the repair crew's work, the documents they had prepared, and the damaged equipment stacked in the garage (which I had since replaced), and signed the paperwork agreeing to the amount of their liability. It was a short, pleasant visit. Imagine my surprise when just a few days later I received a letter from the company stating that the inspector had found everything in working order, thus they were denying my claim.

Eventually, another manager sorted through the maze of errors. He personally visited our home to deliver a check and convey his sincere regret for our bad experiences. He candidly shared how my story was becoming a more common scenario and that it troubled him deeply. He was clearly a person who wanted to keep the company's promise and I knew it was people like him and the faithful repair crew who were holding their business together, providing good service, and creating a profit, in spite of their colleagues' failures. Yet for both them and customers like me, lightning was striking again, and again, and again, each day, exhausting our patience, draining our hope, and slowly undermining the strength of our economy. I have talked with people in virtually every field of endeavor who endure the same futility as they try to keep the promises they have made.

There must be a fundamental change in the way we approach these problems. We've got to stop patching up the holes in our management systems and rekindle the fire of a Zero Defects attitude. Then we can restore the values and principles that once made our people and processes reliable.

KEEPING THE PROMISE

KEEPING THE PROMISE

CHAPTER 3
ESTABLISH RELIABLE PROCESSES

☛ Promise

☛ ZD Attitude

☛ ZD Processes

We recognize that we must spend the time, effort, and resources both individually and corporately to organize, document, and implement Zero Defects processes to support our Zero Defects attitude.

There is no mystery to establishing reliable processes. It is hard work, but the educational technologies and concepts that allow us to effectively manage processes have been developed and refined by people whose names are familiar to every business person. W. Edwards Deming, Philip Crosby, Peter Drucker, Tom Peters, and the dozens of us who have followed in their footsteps have proven the reliability of the process management fundamentals in virtually every sector of the economy and every possible venue. For almost fifty years we have said that "quality" is defined by the customer's requirements; and that the easiest and cheapest way to limit the number of errors in a process is to prevent them from happening, not clean up after they occur. By breaking down every product or service process into its individual steps and fine-tuning the interaction of our resources and procedures, we can do all things better. And we can teach the principles of process management to anyone who wants to use them, at home or at work. In every generation, these concepts are redesigned and upgraded by new leaders and modernized by language for one common purpose: keeping the promise.

July 16, 1969 is a day that I will always remember. As a young associate engineer on the Apollo launch team, I had watched with envy as previous flight crews walked out of that familiar doorway just below my office window and into their waiting motor-home for the ride to the launch pad several miles away. The excitement and anxiety that pulsed through the members of the launch team can only be described as "game-day." As I walked excitedly down the hallway toward the engineering office I met my boss coming the other way. When he saw me, a big smile broadened his face and he said, "You're just the person I wanted to see." Those words usually meant that he wanted something expedited and I was always eager to serve the "super-specialists." They were a team of twelve state-of-the-art engineers who were the best in their fields. They really knew how to do things right and I had been assigned to them as a data analyst and general, all-around "go-for." He reached into his pocket and pulled out a white plastic-coated card emprinted with the words "Apollo 11 Launch Crew VIP" and said, "If I gave this to you for a few hours what would you do with it?" With that card and the color code on my security badge I could, subject to the need to be there, go absolutely anywhere there were flight operations. My heart leaped and as I reached for the card I said, "I know exactly what to do with this card; see you later!"

I wanted to get as close to the launch as possible, so I headed for the VAB and the special VIP viewing area. I walked on past the reviewing stands, trying to remain calm and nonchalant as various security officers glanced at the security badge and VIP card now hanging from my shirt pocket. I kept thinking "absolutely anywhere" as I continued walking down the dusty road leading to the launch pad and right up to the fire trucks, the closest anyone could be to the launch. I got a lot of funny looks from the firemen, but I said nothing and stopped short of getting close enough to talk to anyone. Being there was surreal, and just moments after I arrived at the fire trucks, the bright flash of the rocket engines ignited with an indescribable fury that shook the ground like an earthquake. The deep power of the vibration caused my clothes to flap and wave on my body in a windless rhythmic dance. My legs felt weakened and immobile as they wobbled in sync with the ground. It was an astonishing moment, both exhilarating and terrifying!

Just as the Saturn V rocket cleared the launch tower I had this amazing revelation: That fiery projectile and its precious cargo was the result of millions upon millions of individual actions and tasks that were done right. As the spacecraft hurtled into space there were millions more electrical pulses and other events happening at billionth-of-a-second speed that all had to work in near-perfect sequence for several days in succession for the Apollo 11 crew to safely reach and return from the moon. And it had been done by people like me—average people, who were willing to submit themselves to the discipline and accountability of simple process management concepts. There were only a handful of scientists and engineers who could be categorized as "super-specialists." The rest of us were average people working with a Zero Defects heart attitude and the ethical restraint common to our generation. Really, all things were possible!

The Ebb and Flow of Ethics

Just as there is an ebb and flow in all economic and social systems, so there is an ebb and flow in process management. At the end of the day, process management is much more of a socio-economic problem than it is an engineering problem. No matter how well the process is designed, the money and people must be carefully managed to achieve success. During the Apollo years, the standard of the NASA engineers who had the final authority for the program was clear and simple. It was a NASA rocket and spacecraft. NASA paid for it, they owned it, and they would make the decision to launch. But, they would not launch any vehicle *until the contractors were able to prove to them that they could launch and recover the crew safely.* This was a reasonable balance of power and moral-restraint that we could all live with; and it worked. NASA launched and recovered six successful moon missions and salvaged a seventh, Apollo 13, which many believe was an even greater accomplishment.

But by the morning of January 28, 1986, the day of the Space Shuttle Challenger tragedy, NASA's attitude had changed. In summary, they said something like this in the arguments that took place that morning prior to the launch: *"NASA owns this vehicle and we will launch it when we want."* Notwithstanding the now well-documented protests from respected engineers who were clearly exhibiting a Zero Defects heart attitude, NASA launched what would prove to be a predictable disaster. The ebb and flow that resulted in this historic failure was not one of engineering prowess or process management concepts. It was actually the result of the ebb and flow of ethical standards and the lack of ethical restraint by NASA decision-makers. Now, nearly twenty years later, almost every experienced worker in virtually every field of endeavor can point to a similar change in heart attitude that has dramatically affected their personal or corporate success and unnecessarily harmed people.

A Common Sense Approach

A few years ago I was teaching a seminar on Quality Management principles when someone made this comment: "This stuff is just common sense, and easy to understand." "Yes," I said, "but the magic is not in the knowing; it's in the doing." There was a time when we could teach process management to a group of people and they would simply take what they had learned to their workplace and implement it. That's because the work ethic and disciplines that are required for QM to be successful were more widely shared among coworkers. By the end of their careers, leaders like Deming and Crosby faced a bewildering dilemma. The doctrine they had so long championed was no longer so easily developed. The "cultural change" that they knew was needed had always been similar in difficulty to a face-lift. But now that our ethical framework has deteriorated, it has become more like a heart-lung transplant. The concepts of process management can no longer be taught as a free-standing management doctrine. To be effective, they must be fully integrated with a renewal of vocational and ethical values.

The cultural transformation that is required to support a Zero Defects attitude is a valued-added process—first to every person, then to each process and the products or services it produces, and finally, to each measure of profitability—all for the purpose of fulfilling the promise. From the auto-manufacturer to the social worker, there must be a renewed emphasis on adding value to every person both intellectually and ethically. To do so, we must appeal to those deeply held personal and social motives that easily align themselves with the common sense principles of Quality Management. And we must spend the time that is needed to renew our ethical standards and make sure that we share common values for vocational excellence, personal reliability, and the reasonable use of authority. The next three chapters describe how to achieve these goals.

KEEPING THE PROMISE

KEEPING THE PROMISE

CHAPTER 4
ENCOURAGE VOCATIONAL EXCELLENCE

☛ Promise

☛ ZD Attitude

☛ ZD Processes

☛ Vocational Values

We also recognize that unless we share common values for vocational excellence and can have reasonable and reliable conversations with one another that we will be unable to produce Zero Defects processes. Those values are Vocational Certainty, Process Quality, Administrative Consistency, and Executive Credibility.

PART I – VOCATIONAL CERTAINTY: A MEASURE OF OUR FAITHFULNESS TO OUR AGENDA

I often hear people complain about having to attend meetings where nothing is accomplished. This is especially troublesome when the meeting agenda is to improve the design of a product or service, or to eliminate a known problem in a process, but instead is dominated by useless discussions that resolve nothing. That's the kind of experience you can expect when people try to discover a reasonable solution to a problem that requires accurate, reliable information and clear responses to questions without the benefit of common vocational values to guide them. Vocational certainty requires that we ask these questions of ourselves: Should I be sitting in this particular chair doing this particular job? Should I be involved in this particular discussion? Am I equipped by education and experience to perform effectively the task before me? Often, too many of the people in a meeting can not firmly answer "yes" to these questions.

Make Sure of Your Calling and Vision

Many people, especially in the field of human services, feel called to their work. They know that what they are doing is important and that it fits their skills and personality. To know what job we should be doing, what problems we are capable of solving, or what career path we should be pursuing we have to know who we are. That includes our personality, character, intelligence, talents, education, training, and experience. By honestly comparing our natural talents and interests with the options available to us, it should not be difficult to choose the proper career path or business opportunity. There are also testing and assessment tools that can provide an objective evaluation of these important factors. However, vocational testing is often, but not always, helpful. So having an honest discussion with friends or family may be just as reliable in confirming who we are and what we should be doing.

As a manager, I want to be sure that the people who counsel me and deliver the information I will use to manage processes are filling positions for which they are truly qualified. I will also be concerned about the character of the people who represent me to my employees and customers. When people do not have the right skills for their job, they are tempted to use oppressive methods for getting things done. Vengeful, retaliatory behavior is most often associated with people who lack the vocational certainty to do their jobs the right way, while a pleasant, helpful attitude is more likely an indicator of the quiet confidence that accompanies vocational certainty.

Some of the greatest heartbreaks I have witnessed took place because a leader had not thoroughly tested and proven the skills and character of fellow managers or leaders before they were allowed to act on his or her behalf. It's a frightening thing to sit in a meeting with a leader who has no idea how poorly a staff member is serving their agenda because the leader has failed to discover what others in the room already know—that the staff member lacks vocational certainty. The only thing that could be more troubling is for the leader to be the only person in the room without vocational certainty. Occasionally, because of social or political factors, people get promoted to jobs which do not properly reflect their strengths. And just as often, a person's vocational certainty may have gone unchallenged until they reached a position with enough power to discourage anyone from further questioning. Eventually though, all these things come to light and it is better to find vocational certainty under the power of your own will than under the glaring light of failure.

As a customer, when someone presents facts to me about a product or service that I am considering, I want to be sure of the person's vocational certainty. As a potential employee, I want to be as sure as I can of the vocational certainty of the people I may be joining. If someone is trying to motivate me to take action on a particular agenda, I want to know if their facts are dependable and whether their vision is the result of vocational certainty or was produced by misplaced zeal. People who experience failed visions or career troubles are often distracted by things that do not confirm vocational certainty, instead allowing personality to trump credibility when choosing whom to rely upon for facts.

Imagine that tomorrow you must attempt to design or repair important product or service processes with colleagues who have occasionally caused you to have doubts about their vocational certainty. How confident would you be that you could have reasonable and reliable conversations that would result in effectively designed solutions? And what if you have personal knowledge about one or more of your colleagues that cause you to doubt their honesty or their ability to maintain confidentiality? How comfortable would you feel discussing sensitive planning and budgeting details with them? Have you ever calculated how much extra time and effort is required to have what ought to be simple, clear, and direct conversations because of these kinds of issues? Have you ever considered how, like lightning striking again and again, these things interfere with or prevent you from being able to effectively fulfill your promises? That is why the vocational and ethical values described in these chapters are so important. When they are absent from our routines and relationships, they are a constant threat to our keeping the promise.

Commit to Personal Excellence

Success at work greatly depends upon a person's ability to perform with excellence and fulfill his or her promises to a customer or employer. That means we must be willing to do what is necessary to prepare ourselves. For the majority of my adult life I have been involved in various human services and helping professions. There are always a lot of unknowns to be discovered when we are helping people with problems, but fortunately, I began my career in an engineering environment which demanded accuracy and precision. I worked for twelve engineers in the Apollo program who made decisions based upon a search for what was true and right. They trained me to dig for facts, researching and rechecking my viewpoint until my level of confidence about the right solution would support an effective action. They made serious engineering and flight safety decisions with remarkable precision because they were the best prepared, most disciplined people in their specialties. Watching and listening to them, I realized that people could make good decisions and succeed in any profession if they had enough reliable information. Their example taught me about the power of attaining knowledge and motivated me to set higher goals for my own life and work.

But sometimes our inspiration lacks the planning or self-discipline required to be successful and we need some help. Dr. Bob Hedrick was the Dean of the college where I was taking evening classes to finish my degree. I had arrived early one evening and was on my way to class for a little last-minute cramming when I noticed Dr. Hedrick waiving to me from his office. A retired aerospace executive, Bob had taken an interest in my educational goals and had become a friend and counselor. He knew I was motivated to learn, but that I had also become frustrated at the obstacles I had encountered to furthering my education. I followed him into his office and sat down on the comfortable leather couch across from his desk. He looked really serious, leaned forward across the little table where he had set up coffee and asked, "Larry, are managers born or made?" Surprised by his question, I pondered for a few seconds and then answered, "Born." "Yes," he said, "And you are a natural-born manager. But do you want to die a bitter, old man who didn't get the opportunities he deserved?" I was dumfounded and couldn't think of anything to say but, "No, of course not!" "Well then," he said, "I'm going to help you get the right credentials so that you don't end up that way. You are a gifted young man, but you need some help if you're going to succeed."

The time Dr. Hedrick spent with me that night significantly impacted my life. He eventually helped me lay out and execute reasonable plans for my educational path. He counseled, encouraged, and supported me in ways that I often didn't know I needed until he brought them to my attention. He was a reliable mentor who shepherded my educational experience and added value to my life without trying to squeeze any personal benefit from our relationship. He had committed himself to encouraging young managers to achieve excellence and believed that if he did so generously, he would fulfill his own calling and prosper as an educator.

More than ever, we need people like Dr. Hedrick in every sector of our economy, setting standards for excellence and then helping people achieve them. Both my consulting work and experiences as a customer have given me a startling perspective on how the failure of our educational systems and the erosion of ethics have contributed to the devaluation of personal excellence in America.

One company I visited had forecast that they would need an additional two thousand people to keep up with the growth of their market share. They were an older, established company with their corporate offices in a major metropolitan area. Their community relations staff had convinced them that they could fulfill their goals and help the community they served by hiring young, entry-level people who had been "disenfranchised" by society. It would be an act of "enlightened self-interest" in which everyone involved would benefit.

But it was an exasperating experience for the benevolent-minded company. They were shocked to discover just how "disenfranchised" these young people had become. After interviewing more than ten thousand applicants over the age of eighteen, they were unable to find enough applicants who could pass a minimum standard for literacy and a drug test to fulfill even a fraction of their plans. Before they could send their young candidates to a training program to learn their jobs, they would have to teach them to read and write, use a computer for something other than games, and help them develop the life-skills necessary to stay drug-free and function reliably. It was a disturbing look into the deterioration of our intellectual and ethical infrastructure, but it also explains some of the experiences we are having as customers. Many businesses are forced to "work with what is available." We need to expect more from our families, educators, and public institutions if we are going to recover from this decline. There is nothing more debilitating to individuals and to society at large, than to believe excellence doesn't matter in the culture or environment in which we endeavor.

Develop the Skills to Manage Processes

In addition to producing a marketable product or service, in today's business climate you must also be prepared to manage the increasing legal risks associated with success. What you might think are routine personnel matters can spiral out of control because of a society conditioned to super-sensitivity on discrimination, human rights, and a myriad of other social issues. There is a legitimate need to reasonably protect individual rights in the marketplace. And, all businesses should be held accountable for negligent acts or when a customer suffers unreasonable harm or loss caused by the failure of a product or service. But these important issues are often magnified out of proportion by the over-heated legal rhetoric of greedy lawyers masquerading as good guys eager to defend the oppressed. No matter how trivial the incident, as long as the potential target is a profitable businessperson or entity, somewhere there is a lawyer ready to exercise his or her perverted concept of enterprise and litigate for billable hours, expenses, and a healthy percentage of the settlement.

As difficult as it may be to do our jobs, alert managers must also be prepared to overcome the actions of dishonest employees who will say or do anything to defend themselves from accountability, dishonest customers who will say or do anything to gain a financial advantage to which they feel entitled, dishonest suppliers who will say or do anything to dodge the responsibility of their errors, and so on—lightning striking again and again, and often aided by dishonest lawyers who will say or do . . . well, you get the picture. The ethical failure of the legal sector has fueled the desires of a society with far too many people who are willing to say or do anything to get their own way, making it far too difficult for an honest person to perform his or her duties. But for the truly honest manager, there is a simple path of escape from this maze of deceit. It is found in three principles which are commonly associated with the legal and fiduciary responsibilities of managing people and processes. They are: discovery, due diligence, and reasonableness.

1. The principle of "discovery" is best described as the point in time when we become legally responsible as individuals and managers. It takes place at the moment we "discover" a fact or event. You might see and hear the event yourself; or it might be reported to you by a reasonably reliable source. And in some cases, you might be held responsible for something you could have reasonably been expected to have known.

For example, if a nurse fails to show up for work and does not call his manager to explain why he will be absent (a no-show/no-call), the nurse-manager should be expected, as a reasonable part of her duties in preparing the nursing staff for their shift, to "discover" that the nurse was absent and make arrangements for someone to cover his duties. So if an error or accident takes place on the no-show/no-call's shift that can be traced to the absence of the errant nurse and the failure to redistribute his duties, the nurse-manager could not reasonably expect to escape liability by claiming that she "did not know" the nurse was absent.

2. The principle of "due diligence" is best defined as giving every fact, event, issue or problem the "diligence" it is "due." This is a judgment call based upon what actions should reasonably be expected of a person who was being diligent to fulfill his or her duties.

Continuing with our no-show/no-call example, if the nurse-manager had "discovered" the nurse's absence within a reasonable period of time, immediately assigned another nurse to cover his duties, requested a replacement from her staffing source, and began regular follow-ups to be certain the absent nurse's duties were being covered; she could reasonably be described as acting with "due diligence." Thus, if an error or accident takes place with one of the patients that would have been assigned to the no-show/no-call nurse, the nurse-manager would not be reasonably expected to have liability related to the absence.

3. The principle of "reasonableness" is best described as the measure by which we determine whether or not a person's actions are appropriate for the circumstance. In other words, is the action taken relative to what a reasonable person might do in the same situation? Notice how many times a form

of the word "reasonable" was used in our nurse-manager scenario.

But how can the nurse-manager reasonably prove how and when she "discovered" the no-show/no-call, and whether or not her actions were consistent with "due diligence?" Her case might have been easily resolved if she had been routinely keeping a C.E.N. (pronounced "sin") Journal of significant workplace events *as they occurred.* In both law and management, a *"contemporary extemporaneous note"* is recognized to be the most powerful method for initially documenting facts and events. It is an *immediate* record, written at the time of "discovery" that explains our observations and actions. By accurately journaling the date, time, and relevant details, we can provide a baseline of information from which others can decide whether our actions were consistent with what a reasonably diligent person might do in the same situation. I have accumulated dozens of stories where a C.E.N. Journal has turned what could have become a tragically unfair situation into a clear defense for the accused. For the person who is not too proud to carry a tiny spiral notebook in his or her pocket and not too reluctant to be seen as a "note-writer," it could easily become a career-saver.

Press Toward Continuous Improvement

Our success in managing processes has more to do with people's motivation than it does with resources and other tangibles. So when we set standards, they should be tempered with some understanding of the people who are to perform duties and services on our behalf. I once read an article that criticized what the writer called the "motivational" aspect of QM. He thought that many of the meetings and discussions he had observed in QM work places were unnecessary. He believed that people were motivated by work itself, along with their need for money. It was his opinion that we should allow competition and people's fear of losing their jobs to cause them to perform to higher standards.

This man's work philosophy reduced the motivation of the average employee to a rat in one of B.F. Skinner's experiments (1953), feverishly pulling a lever to receive a food pellet, or in this case, the money needed to survive. Of course, the writer was correct in that most people's motivation for working is to support themselves and their families. But people are also motivated by more idealistic values. Very few people can work effectively for extended periods of time without knowing the strategic purpose of their labor, and what difference, if any, it will make in the world. People want to know that the things they are attempting are doable. If there is a risk, they want to know what it is and how it might affect them. They also want to know the potential rewards.

The writer of the article did not understand how QM created the enthusiasm to improve products and services in the companies he observed. The desire to improve was not caused by pep talks and motivational techniques, but by the hard work of answering people's questions and taking an interest in them. This kind of leadership is considered boring and a waste of time by those who do not understand its importance, but a direct line can be drawn between helping people see the values that are being fulfilled in their work and their motivation. When people are motivated, they naturally reach for higher levels of effectiveness or productivity and will embrace new and higher standards.

One of the best examples of how and why people are motivated is found in a classic of management literature, the Hawthorne Studies. Western Electric, the research and manufacturing arm of the Bell companies before their breakup and now a part of Lucent Technologies, has a reputation for the highest standards in telecommunications, research, and manufacturing. The employees of its Hawthorne plant have been the subjects of studies in human behavior and industrial psychology since the 1920's (Roethlisberger and Dickson, 1943). In one study, the experimenters wanted to measure the effect of environmental factors on the productivity of assembly line workers. The scenario went something like this: They decided to improve the lighting in a particular assembly room to determine its effect on productivity. They installed extra lighting and then over a given period of time they measured the productivity of this particular unit. The result was a specific percentage of increase.

Then they decided to change the chairs used by some assemblers and install a more comfortable model. As before, they obtained a measurable increase in productivity. Then they decided to reconfigure one of the production areas, giving each assembler a more comfortable work space. Again, they measured a specific increase in productivity. In order to validate the cause and effect of the improvements, they decided to reduce the lighting back to its original intensity and measure the decrease in productivity. To their surprise, they measured another increase in productivity, not a decrease as they expected. The same result occurred when each experiment was reversed.

Puzzled by the outcomes, each of the assemblers was asked to participate in extensive interviews and evaluations. They discovered that the increases in production were related to the motivation of the employees. However, their motivation was not related to the improvements, which they then knew statistically from the results of removing them. The interviews proved that the employee's increased motivation and productivity were related to personal factors such as their perception that they were getting personal attention, their feelings of importance as the objects of the study, and having their comfort considered by their superiors. This has become known as the "Hawthorne Effect." When we include people in design and decision processes, provide them with training, equipment, and supplies, or respond to their personal or professional needs, good things happen.

The system that drives QM is prevention. This important concept is directly related to establishing standards for quality because it challenges us to answer the question: How many errors and defects are too many? Remember the hamburger story? The only reasonable standard for prevention is expressed by the term "Zero Defects." The standard of Zero Defects is not a demand to achieve perfection, but, both personally and professionally, it is the only standard that achieves continuous improvement. When people are complacent about defects in their personal life, family, or business, they are not able to reach their potential for improvement. But some people have tried to rationalize away the inaccurately inferred demands of a Zero Defects standard by establishing what are called "Acceptable Quality Levels" (AQL). The primary motivation for an AQL is to lessen the perceived threat of a standard of perfection.

I was taking questions following a lecture about process management when one of the participants asked the ultimate Zero Defects question. It was posed by the administrator of a nonprofit medical institution which treated newborn babies in physical crisis. She described the incredible commitment of her co-workers and the heart-rending decisions they made day after day and literally minute by minute, trying to save the lives of the little children in their care. She tearfully expressed that it was already their desire to fulfill the medical requirements of every baby, every time; yet there was nothing they could do to prevent the death of some of those babies. She wanted to know how a commitment to Zero Defects would help their situation.

First, I reminded her that we all understood she and her co-workers could not be perfect and save every baby. However, it was possible for them to manage their resources and processes so carefully that no known method or procedure was left untried, and that nothing they did contributed to the loss of a baby. In fact, by her description, it sounded as though they had a Zero Defects attitude already, if not a Zero Defects process. She expressed relief and hope because of my response, but her reaction would have been very different if I had encouraged her to establish an Acceptable Quality Level (AQL).

Setting an AQL is intended to take the pressure off people, so they can improve incrementally. You set a performance standard you can live with such as 80 correct actions out of 100, reach it, raise it again to maybe 85, reach it, raise it, etc. Since most improvement comes incrementally, this sounds reasonable. Unfortunately, continuous and incremental improvement will not occur without a commitment to Zero Defects, which is 100 correct actions per 100 attempts. Here is why: It is impossible for anyone to preset a specific number of mistakes they will make per one hundred repetitions of any action. The more we try to count mistakes as we work and adjust our performance, the more mistakes we make. The only way to constantly improve is to attempt to prevent all errors. Afterwards, we can check for errors and count them. Our progress will then be incremental and continuous: 80, 85, 90, etc.

As an example, suppose we pick an AQL of 90%. This means that we want to do things right the first time 90 times out of 100 or the converse is to make 10 mistakes out of 100 attempts. A simple four step process with a 90% AQL will result in an average rate of effectiveness of 58%, or 42 errors in every 100 attempts at the process. This is calculated exponentially by multiplying each step by the factor of .90. Step 1: 100 x .90 = 90%. Step 2: 90 x .90 = 81%. Step 3: 81 x .90 = 73%. Step 4: 73 x .90 = 58%. These are the results that will occur if you are successful in achieving an AQL of only 10 mistakes out of each 100 attempts at each step of the process. In other words, 42 out of each 100 customers will receive some defect because of a preset defect rate of 10 per 100. Whether you count those defects in medical services, books, or sandwiches, the results are not very appealing.

Measure Your Performance Accurately

The quality of the products or services produced by a process is measured by the price of non-conformance—what it costs in dollars and human values when we do things wrong. The price of non-conformance is determined by calculating how much money we spend in rework or repair, problem-solving, client loss, and a myriad of other factors which cost us money and credibility when we make mistakes. Recovering lost profits and improving customer satisfaction should be sufficient motivation for most people to seek improvements in their work. But because of the discipline required to implement the fundamentals of process management, we can easily become sidetracked into inaction. Usually, something has to happen to emphasize the risks and rewards, and help us move from theory to practice.

I began working on the Apollo program only a few months after the tragedy of Apollo 1 when astronauts Gus Grissom, Ed White, and Roger Chaffee lost their lives in a fiery inferno during a launch countdown rehearsal. In a full launch rehearsal, virtually everything is prepared the same as it will be on launch day. All the systems are fueled and "powered up" into full operation. It is a very serious exercise that challenges every aspect of the launch team, crew, equipment, and support personnel around the world just days prior to the actual launch. The Apollo 1 crew and team could not have anticipated that on this particular day, two apparently unrelated design changes would present the opportunity for two simple mistakes to result in tragedy.

First, a design change had been made to use a single gas atmosphere of oxygen within the spacecraft itself, instead of the normal two gas mix of oxygen and nitrogen. This would lower the complexity of various valves and pipes, and reduce the weight and space required to store the gases in the service module of the spacecraft. Although it simplified the process, it also slightly increased the risks. Pure oxygen, while not flammable by itself, enhances the burn rate of other materials.

Second, a new outward-hinged hatch design had been approved, but had not yet been installed. The hatch on the spacecraft hinged inward instead of outward to take advantage of natural pressures within the spacecraft. This helped keep the "front door" tightly sealed. But this arrangement also made escape much more difficult, and under the high pressures of an oxygen-aided fire, made escape impossible.

At some time during the preparation of the spacecraft, two critical mistakes were made. As a flight control panel was installed, the insulation was accidentally peeled back from a wire, leaving it vulnerable to an electrical short and arc. Additionally, a technician inadvertently left a tool behind that same panel which lodged against the exposed wire and created the potential for an inferno. During the launch rehearsal, one of the astronauts routinely changed a switch position on the fully powered panel, creating a spark between the exposed wire and the tool. The spark ignited the peeled-back insulation and then fire engulfed the inside of the spacecraft.

Each factor raised the risk of a disaster, but no one could have guessed they would all come together to create one. The price of non-conformance included the loss of three astronauts' lives and devastation to their families, injuries to several technicians on the launch tower, psychological trauma to hundreds of support personnel, the destruction of a spacecraft, damage to the launch tower and support systems, and congressional investigations that threatened the future of the space program. The jobs of literally tens of thousands of people were in jeopardy. And the financial losses were tens of millions of dollars, all because of an installation error and the misplacement of a two dollar tool.

When I became a member of the launch team, I was lectured extensively on safety procedures and the consequences of mistakes by people only remotely related to the actual spacecraft. My orientation included a tour of some of the more sensitive areas and I was taken into one of the "clean" rooms where a spacecraft was being prepared prior to being placed upon the launch vehicle. I was escorted up a short flight of stairs onto a platform which held the beautiful little capsule snugly and safely away from danger. On the floor of the platform, a two-inch red line was painted in a three-foot circle around the spacecraft. I was told that crossing that red line without the proper authorization and an approved list of every tool or object you took inside, so it could be checked when you came out, would result in immediate dismissal. I would never have the need to cross that line, but they meant business, and a visit to this room sent a clear message to everyone to do things right the first time, wherever they worked in the program.

Experienced process managers know that little mistakes can cause big losses. And the biggest "little mistake" a company can make is losing its perspective on executive accountability. Over the years, I have seen this truth repeatedly confirmed as people failed to take seriously the importance of vocational certainty and the effect that their leadership errors could be having on their staff and customers. This scenario is most prevalent in emerging industries that have enjoyed unusual financial success because of short-term demand for a product or service that exceeds the supply.

Companies whose profits are absorbed by excessive salaries, bonuses, unusually-high dividend rates, or lavish corporate lifestyles have often taken their financial success for granted while failing to upgrade and replace their organizational infrastructure. Seduced by the success of their financial reports, they begin to take themselves so seriously that they fail to hold themselves reasonably accountable, resting proudly on their laurels. As do many businesses, they may be counting the number of people they are able to draw through the front doors and how much money they are making, not how many errors are being made that affect their staff and customers. Being seduced by success can cause people to excuse errors instead of correcting them. It can create a smug bureaucratic attitude which resists listening to reason or honestly measuring performance. Even worse, it can lead to the deliberate manipulation of facts and figures; but eventually the price of non-conformance will prevail. Even then, as the numbers decline, managers can be so deceived by their past success that they continue blindly on until they lose their momentum and run out of money.

The most accurate measurement of our performance is found in a calculation known as "the cost of quality"—what it costs to do things right. It is assessed by comparing the "price of non-conformance"—the losses that are caused by errors, to the "price of conformance"—what it will cost to prevent the errors and do things right. The price of conformance includes the cost of taking bad things out of a process through inspections, audits, etc., and the cost of putting good things into a process, like human resources, benefits, written procedures, equipment, training, etc. When we deduct the one-time and continuing expenses for preventing errors from our potential losses, it usually results in financial gains. This is why Philip Crosby said, "Quality is Free" (1979).

From the steps taken in defining our calling and vision, to the actions that bring them to fulfillment, there are simple values and strategies that determine the outcomes of our work. Each time we establish a reliable value or implement a proven strategy, the certainty of our success is increased.

PART II – PROCESS QUALITY:
A MEASURE OF OUR MASTERY
OF PLANNING AND BUDGETING

A statistics professor once told my class that learning the essentials in any field of discipline amounts to about ten percent of what there is to know. And, that if you had an accurate working knowledge of that essential ten percent, that you would know more about the topic than almost anyone you would encounter at a cocktail party. It was on the basis of this theory that he engaged us into learning ten percent of what there was to know about statistics and learning it well. His goal was not to make each of us statisticians, but to bring us to a level of comfort about the gathering and analysis of statistics so that we could have a reasonable conversation with a statistician, engineer, social scientist, or marketing specialist without embarrassing ourselves. For those of us who were not "technical" people, his exhortation came as a welcome relief. Our goal was to attain a level of competency that could be applied easily and directly to our individual vocations.

Learn the Essentials of Quality Management (QM)

Even though most of us have heard the language of Quality Management, or QM, at one time or another, I have found there is a lot of confusion about what it really means. Because of competition within the field of QM, terms like quality improvement, continuous quality, or total quality are often emphasized to distinguish one practitioner from another. But these are simply routine terms which describe QM's various attributes. For example, the purpose of QM is to *improve* the quality of our products and services. It must be done *continuously* every day we open the doors for business, and must *totally* encompass every person and process.

The concept of Quality Control, one of the most common terms in process management, was born in the manufacturing industry and was intended to keep products with defects from reaching a customer. It is often misused as a synonym for Quality Assurance or QM, but like the others, it has a very specific meaning. It consists of methods for inspecting products in their various stages of production to find and correct errors. Quality Control is what the "inspected by" slip represents in that new package of underwear you just bought. Someone checked that particular package of shorts or shirts to make sure they conformed with the manufacturing requirements before they were shipped. When I reviewed the data of how a spacecraft system performed during a test, I was looking for indicators of a malfunction or failure. Any system or component that did not function properly was repaired or replaced.

The objective of Quality Control is taking bad things out of a process. When we audit, inspect, or check for errors, we are controlling the quality of our products or services by searching for things that do not conform to our requirements. They can then be repaired, converted to some other use, or disposed of as waste. These methods translate easily into all work venues. Service or software processes can benefit greatly from Quality Control, whether it is checking the freshness of food at a restaurant, editing a book for errors in grammar, or inspecting a hospital room for cleanliness.

You may have already realized that Quality Control has its limitations. It is too expensive to inspect every single pair of shorts, every single brake job, or every can of soup, everyday. And, even when inspectors and auditors are carefully trained, there can be inconsistency in their judgments and thoroughness. Because of the human factors involved, no matter how many inspectors are placed in a process, we are going to miss some of the errors and defects. It helps to train people to inspect their own work, but ultimately some amount of Quality Control is needed in nearly all processes. The real issue is deciding how much checking we can afford, what method is appropriate, and where to place it in our processes. It was just this dilemma that brought us to the next concept in the discipline of QM.

Quality Assurance is a term used to describe the methods for putting good things into a process, so that we can be assured of its reliability and prevent errors. This concept came from the aerospace industry and reliability engineering. It was the job of reliability engineers to determine the statistical probability of failure in various components, units, and systems. The study of this problem led to some very simple conclusions. Reliability works backwards from the system, to the unit, to the component, and then to the materials of the components. An air conditioning system is reliable if the individual units within the system, such as compressors, are reliable. The individual units are reliable if the components in them, such as switches and bearings, are reliable. The components are reliable if the materials used to produce them are reliable, etc.

From this basic concept, statistical methods were developed which allowed inspectors to certify the reliability of everything from materials to systems by thoroughly testing a random sample of items from each batch, without having to inspect every single material, component, unit, or system. For instance, from a batch of switches, a random sample would be taken and connected to a machine that would turn them on and off until each one failed, carefully counting each flip of the switch. It could be hundreds, thousands, or even millions of repetitions. The reliability rate was determined by calculating the percentage of failures per repetitions.

In the case of aerospace components, the minimum required reliability rate could easily be 999,999 correct functions out of 1,000,000 or even higher, depending on the possible consequences of failure. Using this method, a whole batch would either be certified as reliable for its intended purpose, routed to another use like toaster ovens, or destroyed. Putting good things into a system, such as components certified as reliable, was intended to prevent failures that could have otherwise occurred and "assure" us of our objectives; thus the term Quality Assurance.

It was further discovered that by putting good things into human systems and organizations such as well-researched design requirements, carefully written policies and procedures, the appropriate equipment and supplies, and thorough training, we could increase their reliability. When people know precisely what is expected of them, have what is needed to accomplish the job, and know how to do it, the processes become more reliable and quality is assured. Again, these same principles apply equally in both service and software processes. If we want to be assured of the quality of our counseling services, sales presentations, or hotel operations, we must spend the time and money to put good things into our processes.

QM is the deliberate management of processes, using Quality Control and Quality Assurance methods. Its objective is to take bad things out and put good things into our processes, in order to prevent errors and conform to our customer's requirements.

Organize Ideas into Work Processes

The success of our career is not measured by how many good ideas we have, but by how many of them are accepted and implemented. All of us have had what we thought was a good idea to improve an important process at home or at work. But things don't always work out just the way we envisioned them. Sometimes the flaws in our ideas don't surface until it's too late and we have made a mess. Because of our bad experiences and the fear of failure at work, a lot of good ideas never get presented. And some good ideas get rejected because they are poorly organized or presented. But there is a proven method for organizing our ideas into work processes. Its simple steps provide a reliable framework for evaluating opportunities, organizing projects, and accurately predicting resources before we become over-committed to what may be a bad idea disguised as a good one. Work Process Analysis (WPA) operates on four simple premises:

First, every good idea will ultimately require work of someone. If little Joey has an idea for something good to eat, someone must prepare the food and serve it. If your boss has what he thinks is a good idea for a new sales campaign, someone will have to organize, plan, and execute the idea. Every idea, good or bad, will require work of someone for the idea to become a reality.

Second, all work takes place in segments (or steps) that together are called processes. Almost everything we do at home or at work can be described as a process, with a beginning, end, and logical segments of activity in between. When we cook, mow the lawn, play ball, drive the car, write a proposal, or repair machinery, we are performing the work of an identifiable process.

Third, resources flow through processes to produce specific outcomes. To make a cheese omelet (a specific outcome), someone (a human resource) must acquire some eggs, cooking oil, a frying pan, a stove, plates, utensils, etc. (resources) and combine them using a specific procedure or sequence of steps (process). The design and implementation of every process is controlled by the resources that are available.

Resources Flow Through Processes to Produce Specific Outcomes

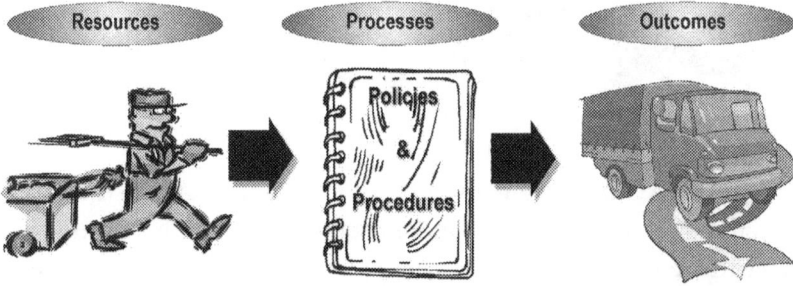

Fourth, each segment or step in a process depends upon the successful completion of the previous steps. If someone mishandles the eggs and drops them on the floor, there will be no omelet. To prevent this kind of error, a better procedure for handling eggs must be developed. When we concentrate on improving the individual segments of a process, we can make the overall process more reliable.

With enough information, anyone can make reliable development decisions, separating valuable opportunities from worthless adventures. Following the simple steps of the WPA method, which is an application of well-known project management principles, we can evaluate any project we might envision by separating it into its logical processes and segments of development and then researching their reliability. The information we accumulate while researching the validity of our ideas can then become the road map for how to do things right. Let's look at each of the steps:

Step 1 – Describe What Needs to Be Done

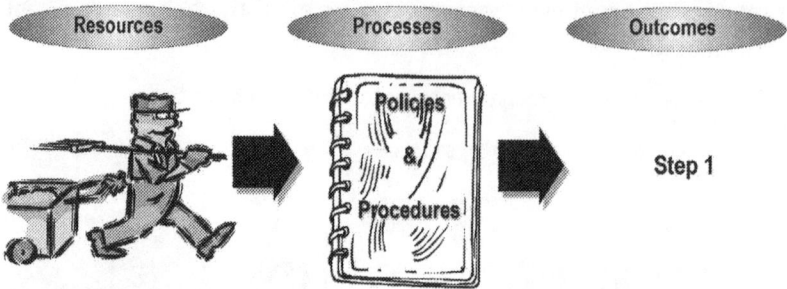

Resources → Processes → Outcomes

Policies & Procedures

Step 1

Before we implement an idea, we must define and research the specific outcomes we envision, and determine whether or not we have the resources to complete the project. Then we can implement our plan with confidence. The desired outcome may be a product, service, or a simple process improvement; but no matter what the goal might be, I think you will find the disciplined organizational approach of WPA very helpful. There are four parts to Step 1:

A. Name the project. In as few words as possible, describe the objective of your project. For example: Making an Omelet. Usually people have grand ideas for the name of their project such as: Making the Perfect Mason-Dixon Vegetable Omelet. But for now, just describe what needs to be done. Don't spend a lot of time laboring on topics related to how marketable your omelet might be until you have completed a few omelets. You might discover important facts as you work through the steps of WPA that will change how you feel about the omelet business.

B. List and describe the key processes that will support the project. This is the beginning of an exercise in list-making. Each step in the WPA method creates opportunities to reexamine the validity of your ideas and rewrite your lists and plans. You will have to make decisions about the amount of detail you include in your lists and when to replace old data with newer more reliable facts. But you must accumulate enough accurate information about each item to make dependable decisions and keep the various sub-processes organized. This step helps you establish reasonable priorities for your planning and research, especially if there are a large number of supporting processes. For example:

Project Name:

Making an Omelet

Key Processes:

1. Choose a recipe and ingredients
2. Determine what appliances and utensils are required
3. Gather or purchase the ingredients, utensils, etc.
4. Prepare and organize the kitchen
5. Cook and serve the omelet

C. List and describe the products or services that will be produced or the actions that will be required. At this point, you should dream and describe ideal versions of what you want to happen. Putting your ideas down on paper and reexamining them causes you to discipline your thoughts and eliminate obvious conflicts, but you should feel no burden to get all the details "right" at this stage of your work. This is a preliminary step in WPA and you are only producing "drafts" of what might ultimately become your project. The details will become clearer as you continue to research and rewrite the requirements. It is quite normal to discover new information or have ideas that cause you to change the elements of a process, product, requirement, or even the central theme of your project. This additional step in formatting your planning list provides another piece of the organizational framework within which you can then fill in the details you will need to be successful:

Project Name:

Making an Omelet

Key Processes/**Products, Services, Actions:**

1. Choose a recipe and ingredients
    A. Western, Southern, or Mason-Dixon
    B. Vegetables, meats, and/or spices
2. Determine what appliances and utensils are required
    A. Pan or other cooking surface
    B. Knives, mixers, etc.
3. Gather or purchase the ingredients, utensils, etc.
    A. On hand in kitchen or borrowed
    B. Shopping list

4. Prepare and organize the kitchen
    A. Clean the cooking utensils and surfaces
    B. Arrange condiments and spices
5. Cook and serve the omelet
    A. Sunday brunch
    B. Invite Joey, Deb, and Sally

D. List and describe the requirements for each product, service, or action. This is another expansion of your list. The details now become more important. You should include factors such as the size, shape, type, anticipated frequency of use, and any other known descriptors. This will be a good test whether or not the knowledge and experience you already have will apply to the project. The number of words you use to describe what needs to be done for each item on your list can vary from a few paragraphs to a few sentences, or, as I have used for these examples, just a few words. Using "enough" but not "too many" words can become a challenging exercise in information management. For example:

Project Name:
    Making an Omelet
Key Processes/Products, Services, Actions/**Requirements**:
    1. Choose a recipe and ingredients
        A. Western, Southern, or Mason-Dixon
            1) Low-fat, digestible, and tasty
            2) No cheeses
        B. Vegetables, meats, and/or spices
            1) Extra-large, fresh eggs
            2) Summer vegetables
            3) Honey-baked ham
    2. Determine what appliances and utensils are required
        A. Pan or other cooking surface
            1) Non-stick skillet
            2) Hot stove-top and microwave
        B. Knives, mixers, etc.
            1) Fine-cut vegetable dicer
            2) High-speed blender

3. Gather or purchase the ingredients, utensils, etc.
    A. On hand in kitchen or borrowed
        1) Borrow Sally's blender, Saturday
        2) Retrieve vegetable dicer from attic
    B. Shopping list
4. Prepare and organize the kitchen
    A. Clean the cooking utensils and surfaces
    B. Arrange condiments and spices
5. Cook and serve the omelet
    A. Sunday brunch
    B. Invite Joey, Deb, and Sally

One of the first things we learn about writing lists is that they often need further refinement. The initial requirements that we can describe may be simpler and then grow in detail. The important lesson here is to remain flexible, yet organized. And, we must be aware of the need for sharing and repeating information in related sections of our list. For instance, we intend to borrow Sally's blender as well as invite her for brunch. So we will need to pick-up the blender on Saturday, avoiding any uncomfortable problems that might occur if Sally is late or unforeseeably absent.

Managing information effectively for a fun project such as this one will be quite easy. But the larger, more complex and important the project, the more difficult it becomes to manage information. That is when spreadsheets and project management software can be helpful. Architects and engineers routinely use this kind of technology to manage the many lists and details of their projects. With these user-friendly computer programs we can easily organize project categories and link them to one another, no matter how large or small the project, and they can be purchased inexpensively at your local computer store.

But even if you are only using a three-ring binder, describing what needs to be done through the simple discipline of "list-making" is essential to the success of any project. Each time we add dependable information to a list, we are reducing the probability of errors and increasing the reliability of our judgment on critical tasks at decisive moments in the development of a project.

Step 2 – Research How to Do It Right

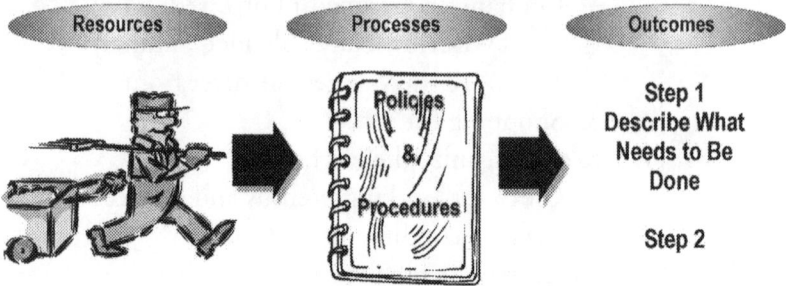

If you were considering a more serious project, you would want to find out what other people think of your ideas. Potential customers, referral agencies, and other parties who may have an interest are interviewed to verify their needs and requirements, and gather suggestions they may offer about your design. A project must be subjected to the scrutiny of potential customers, and the communities that will interact with or regulate its activities. This is very hard work. Doing market research is a little like being a ping-pong ball as you are propelled back and forth by people's conflicting ideas and input. Even the ideas you receive from a single interview can sound like a list of opposing requirements.

A researcher should ask as many pertinent questions as possible; those who do not, often regret it later. Fatigue, excitement, or the fear of rejection, can cause us to stop short of asking the right questions and finding valuable information. You can have what you think are terrific ideas, but the answers that consistently surface are more likely what you need to hear. Both enthusiasm and cynicism can be misleading. You should throw out the high and low responses and listen for the central theme. The objective of research is not to convince others about the viability of your project. You should simply describe your plans and then listen for the data that is needed to succeed. Your research interviews should include:

> 1. Potential clients, customers, or recipients—people who might use your product, service, or participate in the activities you plan. It can be especially helpful to talk with people who have already experienced a need for your product or service, to learn what they like or dislike about your plan.

2. The operators of parallel services—people who interact with your target clients but do not provide your proposed products or services. This could include regulatory agencies, police, teachers, health care workers, etc., who deal with the effect of a person's problems, but are limited by regulation or resources in what they can actually do to help. Your product or service may become a resource to them. If so, they could become "screeners" of potential clients and "centers of influence" for your organization.

3. Potential competitors—people who are providing the same or similar products and services either in your city or another city or state. Your future colleagues can be amazingly open and supportive, especially if they will not be directly competing with you. They may have operational experience and information that is critical to the design of your project.

4. Potential investors, volunteers, and contributors—people who have an interest in your products or services and may also want to participate in financial or operational matters. Your interaction with future supporters of your project while you are in the developmental stages causes them to feel much more a part of the plans you are making. Their interest, or lack of it, will also be helpful to know.

You should share as much about your project as time will allow in each interview. However, it is more important to give each respondent time to evaluate and criticize your plans. A serious researcher encourages respondents to speak freely and carefully draws from their reservoir of experience.

When Step 2 is completed, you will have acquired helpful insight into the design of your products or services, who will purchase them, and what they will pay. You will also have obtained a better understanding of the regulatory requirements. You should not move on to the next step until you have accomplished enough interviews to feel secure about the data you have accumulated. This is a true test for any developer.

Step 3 – Calculate What It Will Cost

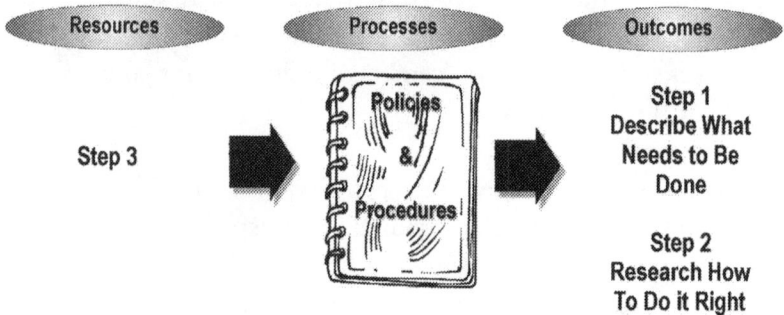

Resources   Processes   Outcomes

Step 3   **Policies & Procedures**

Step 1
Describe What
Needs to Be
Done

Step 2
Research How
To Do it Right

This step of WPA focuses on the production resources required to produce the described outcomes and whether or not a viable budget can be created. Each product or service requires specific human resources, facilities, materials, etc. If you are certain that the product or service you have designed will meet the needs of the clients and the community for which it was intended, you must then determine how many people, places, and things are required to produce it, and what they will cost. Your vision must be relevant to the people and money that is required, and at your disposal, so the following list of action items may be crucial to your success:

> 1. Working from the list of outcome requirements for each product or service, you can define the production requirements (personnel, facilities, equipment, materials, etc.) that will be needed to create those specific outcomes. When this information is gathered, a budget can be produced. This is a critical step in the use of the WPA method, because accurate budget data is essential. You must be able to produce your product or service for less than you expect to receive in sales or contributions in order to keep your project alive and functioning.

56

2. If they are available, at least three sources should be researched for each major item in the budget. First, obtain written bids and then interview each bidder to determine how they produce their goods or services. This will provide comparisons on the competitive advantages one supplier offers over another and a perspective on which supplier will be most reliable. The bid and interview process will also expose you to the business practices and routine communications you can expect to experience as a customer. The lowest price is not always the best bargain in supplier relationships.

3. A major variable in the success of any project is the people. Good relationships with staff members, suppliers, and regulators can have an enormous impact on trust and cooperation when you need it most. So, when possible, spend time with people before you hire them or purchase their services. Talk to them about their values and business philosophy. What you learn in these conversations will provide strategic information for your final decision. The more you know about people, the more accurately you can estimate the costs of doing business with them.

4. After the budget has been constructed in draft form, it should be thoroughly researched to confirm its accuracy. By interviewing potential suppliers, you can re-verify the validity of the production requirements and cost estimations. The availability and lead-time for resources can also be established so that procurement procedures can be planned around reasonable time-lines and cash demands. Adjustments and budget rewrites should be made when necessary.

5. An integral part of budgeting is the computation of production costs and profit margins. The excess between the cost of production and income is called profit, or in the nonprofit world, surplus. The surplus that is available after a business cycle is completed can be distributed for personal gain in a for-profit company. In a nonprofit venture, it must be applied to the purposes of the charter. Reasonably operated enterprises calculate surplus into their production costs and profit margins. When they are not properly computed, there will be no surplus resources to access for production errors, changes in markets, updating infrastructure, or other contingencies.

Step 4 – Decide on a Course of Action

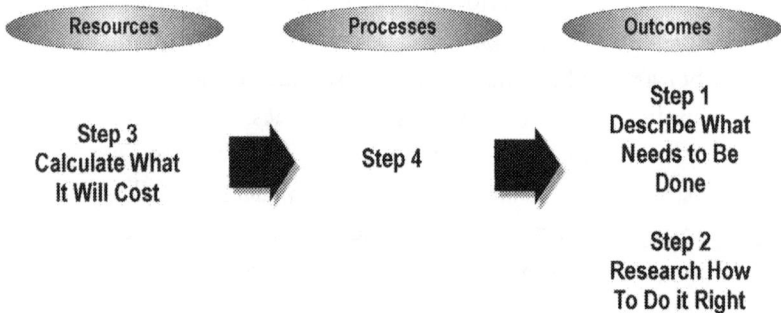

Resources	Processes	Outcomes
Step 3 Calculate What It Will Cost	Step 4	Step 1 Describe What Needs to Be Done
		Step 2 Research How To Do it Right

To help make a correct project decision more certain, you should revisit some previous respondents to your research for a final "reality check." This is an important opportunity to verify the reliability of your project design and retest people's financial interest in your work. Your development options should continue to include redesigning, delaying, implementing, or rejecting the project.

Using the budget as a guide, specific product or service costs should be presented to prospective customers or constituents to test the strength of their interest. Some of these contacts will be repeat interviews, while others should be new contacts, expanding the database for your final decision. The following are a few things to think about as you approach the decision point of your project:

1. The only way you can be sure of a person's interest in your work is to prove its value to them through the sales process. People must be asked to spend their money for your products or services. You must put them in the position to confirm or modify their previous advice by asking for an order (or contribution). What they may have said before could change as they realize you are nearing a final decision. If they will give you an order for your products or services, or make an investment, then their positive comments are believable. If not, their inaction should be considered as a signal to re-evaluate. To make a final decision without testing your constituency in real-life sales conditions is to dangerously presume success.

2. Prospective customers should be consistently positive and willing to buy before you decide to implement your project. If people are reluctant to spend their money, your plans might need to be redesigned or scaled down. Without reasonable financial support, a project's chances for success must be seriously questioned. If prospects hesitate to buy, they should be encouraged to speak freely about their concerns.

3. A researcher can work through each step of the WPA method, rewriting and redesigning his project, and discover that it is enthusiastically accepted. It is also possible to work through all of the steps, with only positive responses until you revisit potential prospects, and then discover that you are not able to finance your project because of the lack of dependable interest. If so, you should be prepared to rewrite your plan, table it until a later date, or walk away satisfied that you discovered its vulnerability.

When I first began my sales career, I remember someone saying, "Nothing happens until somebody sells something." It's true that all products and services require some sales efforts, and the movement of money and resources begins with a sale. Selling is not for the faint of heart, especially if your ability to pay your mortgage is dependent upon the commissions you earned thirty days ago. But sales experience does one important thing for a man—it causes him to be sure of the agreement between the buyer and the seller and not to assume the sale is made until the transaction is complete.

I learned that the success of the sales process depended upon my ability to define the needs of my customer (the outcome requirements), and provide them with an option that fulfilled their desires and their ability to pay. When I had done this well, asking for the order was easier. I could also expect the buyer to feel comfortable with his purchase. But sometimes I asked for the order and found that the buyer was reluctant. When this happened I knew that further discussion was required to determine what buying motives were unsatisfied. Some buyers only need more information, while others balk at the sale because they want a better price, so they fish for negotiating room by criticizing some part of the proposal.

Many people have "great" ideas that will ultimately be accomplished by someone else. If you don't think so, take a look at the storefronts that open and close in your local mall. Ten people can open restaurants and lose their fortunes in the same location. An eleventh can come along with just the right menu and process controls, at just the right time in the marketplace, and make a fortune. In the meantime, the only person making any money is the landlord. The risks of a venture must be soberly compared to our ability to finish the course and our own vocational certainty.

Step 5 - Implement the Work Processes

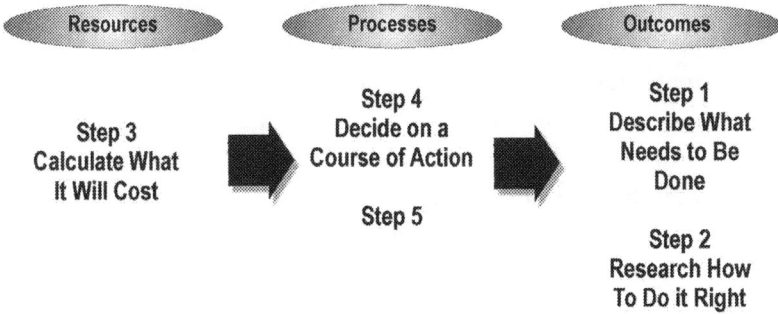

Resources	Processes	Outcomes

Step 3 **Calculate What** **It Will Cost**	**Step 4** **Decide on a** **Course of Action** **Step 5**	**Step 1** **Describe What** **Needs to Be** **Done** **Step 2** **Research How** **To Do it Right**

Once a decision to proceed to implementation has been taken, it is necessary to take the final steps toward organizing your original idea into work processes. Before people will be able to execute the plan on your behalf, they will need clearly written job descriptions, policies, and procedures that explain what, where, when, and how they are to function. Then, each staff member must be given the training and resources they will need to understand and implement the responsibilities of their job description. A fully trained and equipped staff is essential to your success.

There are two dominant sources of errors in project development: 1) the project design and 2) mistakes made during implementation. Because WPA eliminates most design errors, implementation errors are the more common cause of early development failures. The following checkpoints will help you identify and eliminate the remaining sources of errors while they can be inexpensively corrected:

> 1. Write the policies and procedures. A vital task in project development is the conversion of the design and research data that has been accumulated into written policies and procedures. Although it is often regarded as challenging work, the person who has navigated each step of WPA should have little difficulty writing simple instructions about how and when to do things and the resources that will be required.

2. Obtain a short supply of resources. A short supply is the amount needed to turn on and practice the process. This includes people, facilities, equipment, materials etc. For this short period of practice, it is better to buy in small quantities regardless of the unit price. When possible, rent rather than buy and keep inventories at minimums.

3. Thoroughly train the staff. Every dollar you spend in a focused, productive effort to train the people who will operate the processes is an investment in the reliability of the entire project. When the staff executes its responsibilities according to an established set of procedures you can also more easily identify errors in the details of the procedure, the resources provided, the equipment utilized, etc.

4. Turn on the process. The objective is to allow the resources to interact within the confines of the processes to see if they function as designed and described in the policies and procedures. This can take place in a laboratory setting or at an actual location depending upon the type of product or service that will be produced.

5. Perform operations proofing. This step is a combination of quality control and quality assurance actions. We remove bad things from the process (errors) and put in the good things that are required (adjustments to the process, training, etc.). Inspect the interaction of the resources at every step of each process.

6. Obtain customer feedback. When the process appears to conform to the requirements, you may begin delivering the product or service to a customer. The customer's critique at this early stage is vital.

Make him or her feel comfortable describing non-conformances, and be liberal with rework or refunds.

7. Take corrective action. Use the information you have obtained from operations proofing and customer feedback to adjust the processes. Rewrite whatever procedures are necessary and retrain the people who will operate the processes. Keep in mind that this is the most inexpensive opportunity you will have to make these changes.

8. Scale-up the process. This is a judgment call. By now, you will know a lot about your prospects for success. Re-verify the resource budgets, operating expenses, and projected income. Then decide whether to "scale up" operations and create a continuous supply of resources, or return to operations proofing.

As you can see, managing processes so that they produce quality products and services requires a "principled" approach. Although you might not apply each detail of each principle every time you make a decision about an action or project, becoming familiar with these principles and implementing them more frequently into the routines of your work life can have a very positive effect. Imagine that you are the customer. If you were about to make a decision to buy a product or service, approve a project, or hire someone to act on your behalf, which of these principles do you feel can safely be ignored by the person serving you? The answer to that question will help you establish reasonable standards for process quality.

Part III – ADMINISTRATIVE CONSISTENCY: A MEASURE OF OUR ATTENTION TO DETAILS

When people think of Administrative Consistency they often picture a bookkeeper or a shipping clerk sitting in the dusty corner of a back office making sure all of the numbers match on a shipping list. Most leaders would never consider that the way in which they handle simple administrative duties for a customer could propel them into their next level of professional development. Of course, it would depend upon who the customer might be. But if your customer had been Philip Crosby, you would have done well to pay attention to the details he thought were important.

I had known Phil socially for about two years and had enjoyed relaxed lunches with him on a couple of occasions. He was a friendly, yet intense man who had taken an interest in me after hearing me make announcements at a church meeting. Later, when a mutual friend asked me to approach Phil about supporting a philanthropic project he was undertaking, I had my first "business" appointment with him. What was intended to be a brief meeting lasted through much of the afternoon and I left his office with a new respect for who he was, and a new consulting retainer. He wanted me to help him redesign his community relations plan and budgets. He was already doing a lot for the community but wanted to apply the same standards to his giving as he did to his other business processes.

The Gold Is In the Details

A few days later I visited Phil's office to pick up some documents. As I sat waiting for his assistant to finish a telephone conversation, I overheard a very important detail: "I can't give you an hour-long appointment. Mr. Crosby would not allow it. If you can't explain what you need in a few minutes you are not prepared for the meeting." When she hung up she reached into her desk and pulled out the file I needed. As I sat next to her reading the documents, I realized I needed to ask some questions that only Phil could answer. "This might not be a good time." I said, "But I really need to ask

Mr. Crosby about three important items in this file. Could you schedule five minutes for me to see him?" She looked at me in disbelief and said, "Five minutes? You're kidding, right?" "No," I answered, "I will be in and out in five minutes." She smiled, laughed a little under her breath, and gave me a fifteen minute slot for the next morning.

I arrived early. After greeting me, his assistant said, "Remember, only fifteen minutes." I walked over to her desk and whispered "I know. I only need five." She gave me that unbelieving look again and said, "He is waiting for you, go on in."

We shook hands and sat down at the little round conversational table in the corner of his office. I pulled off my watch, sat it up in front of myself like a monitor, handed him a printed agenda with the three questions on it, and began my meeting. He answered all of my questions in fewer than three minutes. I thanked him and got up to leave. "Wait," he said, "Is that it? Is that all you want?" "Yes sir," I responded, "But, as you can see, you are the only person who could have answered these questions." He continued, "Are you sure that's all you want? Sit down and let's talk for a few minutes." It was a golden moment. I had just invented the five minute interview so that I could serve the man who invented the "elevator speech" the way he wanted to be served. By precisely identifying my customer's requirements and respecting both his time and needs for administrative detail, I had pulled deeply on his Zero Defects heart strings. He became more than a friend and customer; he became a reliable mentor who never failed to take my call or give me time to meet with him. Because he was Philip Crosby, that relationship changed my life. But all customers should be treated exactly the same way, with attention to the details they consider important.

Establish Effective Communications

Before a project can function effectively, we have to establish the relationships and processes required for doing business. Then we have to provide each process with the resources it needs. And to properly oversee our work, we must also communicate with staff, acquire and evaluate production data, identify problems, and create solutions. Every process is defined and managed by information, which is transmitted both verbally and through documents such as policy manuals, memos, purchase orders, expense reports, production schedules, etc. These exchanges of information help us explain what we want accomplished. They let us know what people are doing and why, monitor how resources are being managed, and provide the data and statistics that are crucial to our success. Reliable communications are:

1. Clear and specific to the task. They provide answers to the process questions of what, how much, when, and how, and bring enlightenment that is appropriate to the moment. When we are focused on the processes we manage, we develop special knowledge of how things work and become more aware of how people interact with resources and what they need to do their jobs well. It is this accumulation of knowledge and sensitivity to the dynamics of a process that we call "experience."

2. Accurate, honest, and complete. When we can be trusted to impart the truth in a helpful and practical manner, we will be perceived by others as reliable. But more importantly, we can depend upon our staff to make good decisions and follow through on their commitments in ways that are consistent with how we have trained them.

3. Respectful and exhibit consideration for others. We should never forget that much of our success depends upon how people feel about us as a person. When we are careful not to speak abusively, coarsely, or with inappropriate innuendo we can depend upon people to show respect for our leadership.

4. Prudent and create reliable relationships. Each time a decision is made, it can affect the people and resources of an organization as well as the

market it serves. This is especially the case with changes in policy and procedure. What we say in a personal interview, a planning meeting, or at a casual luncheon with peers, can create ripples of reaction across an entire organization. Even the most confidential communications can find their way into public controversy because of their perceived effect on people.

Perform Each Task with Due Diligence

Sometimes I hear young executives talking about management as though it were an exclusive and mystical power that allows leaders to act quickly and forcefully where others fear to tread. They often give the impression that they are able to snatch reliable solutions out of thin air, thus demonstrating their prowess as executives. But the results these kinds of leaders consistently produce are often quite different. The "gut instinct" they say they are relying upon usually leaves a trail of corporate debris caused by their impulsive, misguided actions. Their real expertise is more likely to be their ability to deflect responsibility for their errors, cover-up their mistakes, and remain in power. They don't appreciate how the diligence of ordinary people raises the level of *assurance* for themselves, their staff, and their customers.

Until a person gains enough knowledge and experience to appreciate the benefits of diligence, he or she might feel uncomfortably bridled by the discipline that is required. This feeling of "backpressure" may cause them to argue against the fundamentals of careful, deliberate management; however, they do so in ignorance. A reliable manager must give each fact, event, issue or problem the "diligence it is due." When they don't, their attitudes toward diligence can be observed in rather obvious ways:

> 1. Do they assume and presume? To assume is to *take for granted as reliable or true, without proof.* To presume is to *assume and take action, without testing for proof.* Think of how often you have heard someone say things that sounded like an excuse. For

instance, "I assumed you knew what I meant," or "I thought you had that covered." Or, how often have you seen that same person completely fooled by someone with a big personality but who is less than honest or competent? If you hear or see these things repeated more than occasionally, you can be sure that the person in question rarely engages in the kinds of detailed discussions that are required to be certain of the facts.

2. How do they test and prove the facts? A test is the *means by which the presence, quality or genuineness of something is determined.* The proof of a matter is in the *facts by which it is established.* A realistic test to establish the facts might be accomplished by a few questions specifically related to what must be proven. However, a conversation about the weather will not suffice for detailed questions related to a person's competency. The person who lacks diligence will also demonstrate that he or she does not enjoy the research required to be certain of the facts. This is sometimes related to a lack of vocational certainty. A number-cruncher may not be able to thoroughly test the facts regarding service processes, while the experienced human services practitioner may lack the financial expertise required to test and prove an idea's validity.

3. Are their stated values and practiced values the same? When leaders say one thing but do another, they undermine people's trust in them. As people lose faith in a person's character or decision-making, they will become less willing to take the risks involved in providing the leader with reliable facts. These growing feelings of mutual alienation also cause the leader who lacks diligence to rely more regularly on exercising the "authority" of his or her

position rather than working hard to be consistent and maintain reliable relationships. This dynamic creates a downward spiral in human relations and work processes. When we say we have faith in something, it means that we are morally persuaded of the truth. When people with a Zero Defects heart attitude are *morally persuaded of the truth*, you will see them diligently taking actions that are consistent with what they say they believe.

Monitor Every Process for Defects

Once processes have been established, they must be monitored to make sure they continue to produce actions consistent with their purpose. Processes are dynamic. They are either improving or deteriorating, depending upon the attention we give them. So the pursuit of defects should be a part of our routine if we want to constantly produce quality products or services. Here are a few practical methods:

> 1. Receive and evaluate complaints. Identifying errors can be as easy as receiving customer complaints. When a customer tells us that we have fallen short of our stated values, we should take him or her very seriously. Their advice could help us discover a mistake that is costing us other sales. For every customer who provides negative feedback, there may be many others who quietly find new suppliers.

> 2. Manage by walking around. We can identify non-conforming events by surveying office and production areas and talking to people. Through simple observation of the processes and the people who operate them, and a few moments of relaxed conversation, we can determine whether work areas are clean, organized, and orderly, and identify inter-personal conflicts or cohesion in work relationships.

3. Establish routine process evaluations. Compare the written policies and procedures with what is actually happening. Everything from the materials we receive to the ways we use them should be compared to our requirements for a quality product or service. When the organized pursuit of defects becomes a routine of the work place, people will be less inclined to feel like they are being put under the microscope.

4. Create reliable measurements. By defining "normal" rates of production, costs, or other standards for an event or process, abnormal conditions can be identified as they occur. The types of measurements can range from simple counts of activity by a process during a given period, to errors per hundred events, to the average cost per client, which can be a very revealing measurement.

Master the Art of Delegating Responsibility

Each time we delegate responsibility, we are risking not only the success of our plans, but our reputation. To lower our risk, we must remain close to work processes and hold people reasonably accountable, because our stewardship will be judged by the practices of those acting on our behalf. Sometimes the simple, obvious things are the most important in delegating responsibility. Here are a few reminders:

1. Success often depends upon our ability to choose people who understand our needs and know what has to be done. Smart managers do not want people around them who can only describe problems. They need people who can also solve them.

2. When we delegate process responsibility to people who are unified and coordinated around common goals, the possibilities are nearly limitless.

Unification is obtained as each individual commits himself or herself to the goal. Coordination requires the project to be translated into its fundamental values and strategies.

3. The reasoning that supports our course of action is called "policy." And the steps that will be taken to fulfill the policy is called "procedure." A complete picture of our project is often called a "Policies and Procedures Manual." It includes the specifics of the vision, each person's job description and benefits, and all the processes within the organization. It should answer questions about how and when to do things, and the resources that will be required.

As you can see, the key elements to effective delegation are good people who have a reasonable understanding of their goals. So you must first choose reliable people, and second, provide them with the necessary training and documentation to fulfill the customer's requirements. If you fail to carefully administer each part of this delicate recipe, you are presumptively mixing a formula for failure. However, assuming that you have good policies and procedures in place, the ongoing challenge will be choosing the right people. Just remember:

1. No matter how impressively people are able to present facts and figures or describe the failures of a process, the validity of a person's insight into a problem will ultimately be judged by the wisdom of their solution. There is no substitute for vocational certainty because when a person lacks the specific knowledge or experience required to accurately and effectively resolve an issue, they are unable to add value to a reasonable conversation.

2. No matter how much training a person receives or how well written the policies and procedures, if

he or she is unqualified by personality or character to lead people, the process will suffer. You must be sure of a person's emotional reliability because when you delegate responsibility to someone you expect to be helpful and compassionate, only to discover that he or she is cold and manipulative, you have unnecessarily harmed yourself and others.

Engage in Strategic Record Keeping

Keeping accurate records of the operational and financial activities of an enterprise is a legal necessity. All kinds of reports must be filed with local, state, and federal government agencies. We file forms for everything from taxes to health and safety issues, and the list keeps growing. Filing reports is a reality of doing business, and our failure to perform even perfunctory reporting can carry stiff fines. Fulfilling our legal obligations is reason enough to gather and preserve data, but there are better reasons. An organization must have accurate records to protect its assets and manage its processes. For example:

1. Records that increase our process knowledge are extremely useful for improvement. When we routinely measure and record how much we produce, how many people we serve, etc., we are gathering information that can help us improve processes. When we add to these records financial data such as income per item, expense per item, etc., we are giving ourselves the perspective we need to make better decisions.

2. With all of the challenges in maintaining stewardship within an organization, there are just as many threats from the outside. Procuring products and services can produce a maze of opportunities for both financial losses and errors that can directly impact our processes. Most difficulties with suppliers will be the result of inaccurate clerical operations.

A simple set of records will settle issues which the most principled arguments have been unable to solve and keep vital resources flowing.

3. The systems for keeping records should be designed to anticipate and prevent the common causes of problems—things that can be reasonably predicted to occur. Common causes include such things as errors in orders, billing, payments, receipts, schedules, and other activities which have immediate and direct consequences.

There will always be people who want to take what we have or harm what we are doing. And, occasionally, we will encounter both peers and superiors whose lack of ethical restraint could entangle us in wrongdoing. Sometimes, having a strong personal ethic may not be enough to resist the pressures without creating friction. However, there is a simple technique that will quickly tip the balance of power with a superior who is asking you to take an improper action. It enables you to clearly signal "No" by saying "Yes" with administrative precision. Simply write a note in the person's presence. Be sure to say, as unemotionally as you can, that you want to be sure to have an accurate record of his or her requirements. Ask them to repeat the order so that there will be no mistake in what he or she expects you to do. Then carefully write down everything he or she tells you. Most people will quickly terminate the conversation. Except for a few hardened criminals I have known, people generally have an intense fear about the prospect of someone having a written record of their wrongdoing.

We must always be prepared to take sound administrative action and make an immediate and accurate record of what we see and hear. Remember, when we document and explain our actions in the light of what any reasonable person might do in the same situation, it is called a "contemporary extemporaneous note." Always keep your C.E.N. Journal handy.

Manage Time and Information Wisely

When a situation occurs that is favorable to the attainment of our goals or desires, it is called an "opportunity." Time and information are two of the essential elements of opportunity. If we manage them wisely, we can expect our life to be satisfying and fruitful. The four strategic disciplines of time and information are:

1. Organizing priorities. This is where the elements of time and information intersect most often. Time is precious, and information is often strategic, so it is necessary to decide in advance what requirements will guide our use of them. The activities that support our most important requirements should become our highest priority. We must learn to quickly evaluate activities and data and their value to our requirements.

2. Advancing ideas. This requires the shaping of information and the management of time. Our challenge in life is not how many good ideas we have, but how many of them are heard and accepted. The people who understand this concept will practice shaping what they want to say to the time allotted them, tossing from their presentation anything that is not essential for the listener to make a decision.

3. Problem solving. This process can press the need for accurate information against the urgency of time. An unresolved problem costs time and money, and brings chaos into an otherwise smoothly operating system. While a process is running smoothly, we can ask questions like, "What would happen if this part fails, or this supplier does not deliver, or this person becomes ill?" By establishing contingency plans, we can access resources and information quickly when we need them.

4. Personal growth. This is very often a measurement of how well we have managed time and information. The more effective we become at organizing priorities, advancing ideas, and solving problems, the more mature and experienced we become as managers and handling life in general. These disciplines cross over into every part of our life and create greater and more frequent opportunities.

One of my first assignments in the Apollo program was compiling a list of what test procedures and measurements were needed to assure that each system of the spacecraft was working properly. After it was edited by the engineers who would run the tests, this document controlled what information would be recorded and why. Working from our list and the test results, we knew what was required to be sure that a process was working right. We also knew where to search for the causes of errors. This simple method prepared us to respond quickly to problems and save tremendous amounts of time and money. The efficiencies that were produced also provided our many constituents with the assurances they needed to support our work.

It was during those years that I first started making personal lists and notes, because I was terrified of forgetting an assignment or being asked something I could not answer. When someone gave me a new task or used a term I didn't know, I pulled a small pad from my pocket and wrote it down. I learned to prioritize under pressure and quickly obtain the information I might need in a future conversation. Before long I was not only surviving the stresses of my work, but growing in knowledge and prospering. Those administrative disciplines have helped me to succeed in every venue I have encountered. So when I sat my watch on Philip Crosby's desk, I was applying time and information management skills I had gained many years before.

PART IV – EXECUTIVE CREDIBILITY:
A MEASURE OF OUR
SINCERITY AND SKILL WITH PEOPLE

Tim was the all-American man. He had graduated in the top ten of his class at an Ivy League school, played football in the NFL, and was the CEO of an internationally respected corporation. He loved kids, although he had none of his own, and had worked endlessly to help the poor and disadvantaged children living in his state. His wife was a beautiful debutante who dutifully attended fundraisers and served food at a local soup kitchen alongside her celebrity husband. Tim was generous, friendly, and enormously successful, the kind of person you might expect to enter politics and become governor or even president. He was a huge man and his nickname was "the Bear," a moniker he obviously enjoyed. He knew how to use his hulking physical presence to his advantage, either softening people's defenses by playing the gentle giant or intimidating them into submission with a howling tirade.

You see, the Bear was not at all the person he portrayed in public. When he was behind closed doors with his "inner circle," his warm, fatherly voice could quickly turn cold and vile. He was selfish, demanding, arrogant, and at times, brazenly cruel. His language was laced with profanities and ethnic slurs, and he took sick pleasure in belittling anyone who made mistakes. This was the height of hypocrisy, because Tim's staff kept a secret "clean-up" fund to quietly correct his mistakes. The fund was hidden from the eyes of the shareholders by misnaming line items in the budget.

The Bear's double life was a well-kept secret. By the time most people got close enough to discover his two natures, they had been thoroughly compromised. He had surrounded himself with vice presidents and executive assistants who were willing to be overpaid for their work in exchange for their absolute obedience and silence. They soberly feared what Tim might do to their careers if they ever said or did anything "disloyal," because they had seen many terrifying examples of his vengeful resolve. People who were subjected to Tim's "counsel" often left their meetings paled, confused, and sullen. His staff dreaded even the most routine contact with him, while at the same time, praising his leadership in public.

This Kind of Secret Is Impossible to Keep

Tim's duplicity, although extreme, is not really so rare. You can probably think of someone you have worked with whose leadership skills were rooted in manipulation and deceit rather than sincerity and competence. The cases we have seen publicly prosecuted are more than just metaphors. They are the fruit of a CEO culture that too often believes they are entitled by the "American dream" to live luxuriously and exercise ruthless authority over their shareholder's assets. But no matter how smoothly their public image is crafted, or how loyal their staff, eventually, all unjust tyrants are exposed and "dethroned." It is impossible to keep this kind of secret hidden from constituents, shareholders, customers, suppliers, and eventually reporters or prosecutors. Someone will know, someone will care, and someone will take action.

Like most tyrants, Tim began to indulge his impulses more openly. It wasn't long until the vulgar core of his soul could no longer be shielded from public knowledge. As more and more people outside his inner circle witnessed his abuse, the price of non-conformance became more easily calculated. Finally, a little, frail, bent-over, old man with an antique cane and a quiet, unassuming voice visited Tim's office without appointment. He sat down in Tim's big leather chair, pointed his cane at him and said, "It's over. On behalf of the board of directors, you're fired. Take your things and go." Tim was quietly escorted from the building, saving the company from a public spectacle and continued financial decline. Although the old man was far too late to help the many victims Tim had left brutalized in his wake, as always, someone with credibility had revealed the secret and someone had cared.

Executive credibility is a measure of our sincerity and skill with people, not our ability to manipulate people's perceptions or intimidate them into submission. When people know from personal experience that we are who we say we are and that we will be "just" in the conduct of our business, they are more likely to cooperate with us. But when a leader's credibility is in doubt, people will express their insecurity in ways that are detrimental to the mission. Although tyranny is often credited with short-term success, the price of tyranny is far too high. Eventually, everyone loses, including the tyrant. To gain legitimate influence, leaders must demonstrate emotional maturity along with competence.

Hold People Reasonably Accountable

Those of us who have been abused or humiliated by an authority figure know how our bad experiences can create fears and leave emotional scars that last a lifetime. When people feel insecure or afraid, it leads to serious problems in the work place. But in a *keeping the promise* culture, things are different. For example:

> 1. People are praised and rewarded for finding errors. Knowing this, they will eagerly embrace the search for errors as the path to reaching higher standards. This is especially true when a discovered error is treated as an opportunity to share in the recovery of lost profits.

> 2. People are encouraged to discover and take responsibility for the causes of problems, essentially holding themselves accountable. Other systems of accountability then become secondary and are only needed to separate chronic problems from normal human errors.

> 3. Trust and security are nurtured by having the stated values become the practiced values. But simple consistency by the leaders is not enough. There must also be "due process," with established procedures for gathering and evaluating the facts of an issue and making reasonable judgments.

In a keeping the promise culture, only people who are hardened into dishonest behaviors and unwilling to change should ever need to be fired. Almost any problem can be resolved with honest, well-intended people. But when repeated errors point to a person's attitude instead of simple mistakes or the frailties of a process, the procedures for correction should include progressive discipline.

What appear to be ordinary issues can sometimes require extraordinary effort, especially where tyranny has ruled. People will have to be convinced that it is a new day. They will need to be given both the time and positive experiences that will facilitate their healing and restore them to full productivity. As managers, we might also have to temporarily absorb the consequences of someone's previous bad behaviors so that we are not perceived as just the next tyrant. If tyranny has existed at the top, there will be emerging tyrants scattered throughout an organization who must be carefully identified, evaluated, and challenged to adopt new values. Then, depending upon their ability to change, they can be coached, counseled by a specialist, or terminated. How well we handle these things will be closely watched by both the people who were harmed and those who contributed to the harm.

Cleansing an organization from the effects of tyranny is a time-consuming activity which can not be rushed. It must be supported by a comprehensive training program, roundtable discussions, and individual interviews about the values that will guide the company. But restoring any organization where *any* of the values have been contrary to a keeping the promise culture will require similar elements of activity. It is a fundamental of cultural change—not just recovery from tyranny—that minds and hearts must be won with reasonable arguments.

Avoid the Risks of Becoming Proud

When we violate procedures and misuse power according to our own whim, unfairly hold back approval, promotion, benefits, or subvert due process for our own purposes; it is called tyranny. Tyrants try to make people fear and obey them by emphasizing the harm they might cause. They are tolerated because people fear losing their jobs, financial status, or ranking in a community. When we think about how a tyrant acts or speaks, we associate his or her behaviors with pride. We recognize boasting, arrogance, and heavy-handedness as being the fruit of pride. But beyond that, most people do not understand the potential for pride to stimulate normal people into behaviors that degrade their personality. I have reduced the definition of pride to a few simple operational descriptors:

> 1. Pride causes us to attribute our position or success in life to our own skills, strengths, or righteousness without considering other people's contribution.

> 2. Pride causes us to use our physical, emotional, or mental strength as a weapon to forward our own agenda instead of a tool for the common good or a corporate objective.

> 3. Pride causes us to assume, presume, take things for granted, and forget about process disciplines and good human relations.

> 4. Pride causes us to be angry with other people's limitations and reject the people or things we cannot change. It also produces an inordinate need to control outcomes.

The startling truth is that all tyrants started out as normal people. But along the way they began to accumulate experiences and viewpoints consistent with the four descriptors above. As their bad behaviors turned more deliberate, they consistently justified their attitudes until they were no longer normal people with problems, but tyrants. There is a direct relationship between the tyrant's lack of empathy for people and the unrestricted pride which carries him or her deeper into abhorrent behavior. Eventually, their lack of concern for people's well-being isolates them from reality. They are propelled by their own meanness beyond the ability to change, even as they plunge forward into their own tragic end.

Although almost no one you know will ever reach the levels of a full blown tyrant like Hitler, we would all be wise to avoid the risks of becoming proud. The solution for staying normal is to have lots and lots of accurate information from people we can trust about ourselves and the processes we manage. A tyrant's bad behaviors extinguish most reliable sources of truth, so it is important to surround yourself with reliable relationships, at home and at work, while you're still normal.

Remain Honorable Under Pressure

Most of the bad conduct that we attribute to the stress of the work place can more accurately be traced to either pride or deeply entrenched fears about outcomes. When we believe that the things we have night-sweats about might really be happening, we can become entangled in fear-driven behaviors that cause us to fixate on the worst-case scenario. This "unbelieving" or "negative" point of view creates a narrow, tunnel-vision mentality. It is best described as cynicism or doubt that confuses our perceptions and is often accompanied by outbursts of anger and other unsettling attitudes and behaviors. Fear can create such an unrealistic view of life that it often causes people to place too great a significance on what are really just routine events. As it grows, it fosters unshakeable feelings of dread or insecurity, causing people to have inordinate reactions to even minor problems and feel tortured by what they see as a struggle against unfair pressures. The most common fear-driven behaviors are:

1. Impatience–which is stimulated by the perception that a relationship or process is not going to work out as desired. The result is angry, impulsive behaviors and other expressions of the lack of restraint. Impatient people experience intense anxiety when important or strategic processes appear to be standing still. They fear that inaction will lead to potential problems or failure.

2. Harsh judging–which is often the result of accumulated anger from past events. The pain of past injustices or breaches of trust can cause us to justify our inner feelings of suspicion and doubt. Unchecked, this leads to inaccurate observations,

unfair generalizations, and angry judgments. Harsh judging can surface when we feel socially uncomfortable, limited in our opportunities, interfered with in our plans, or unjustly treated. It is stimulated by the fear that more pain and frustration are imminent.

3. Depression—which can be stimulated by our fear of a potential loss or setback, or the frustration, stress, and fatigue caused by real events. These things can lower our physical or mental state into despondency or moodiness. Feeling the continuous weight of a problem, living with a gloomy outlook, or the nagging feelings of despair can all be indicators of depression. A person suffering from depression might have long periods of inaction followed by sudden and furious attempts at problem-solving.

Left unchallenged, these disruptive behaviors can be the precursor of an emerging tyrant. When organizational authority is given to people who suffer from these maladies, it only intensifies their fears and thus their bad behaviors. So when managers are impatient or harsh, it is a measure of their need for healing, not their strength. As with pride, trying to behave honorably without having good relationships that will provide you with an accurate perspective of your circumstances can be very problematic. But when our fears are legitimately related to a manageable risk, reliable counsel can help us discern our options and craft a reasonable solution.

Discern and Pursue the Just Cause

In the course of fulfilling our routine duties, many decisions have to be made that require wisdom and discerning. To discern means to make a judgment or decide. Typically we make dozens of tiny judgments each day, deciding what to eat, what to wear, where to go, etc. But making judgments is most challenging when our conclusions might affect others. People do not always cooperate, often complicating the simplest issues with their personal biases.

Nonetheless, we must apply ourselves to this important discipline of leadership with the following thoughts in mind:

> 1. Discerning the just cause could be as personal as knowing which house to buy, or as public as deciding what is equitable and fair in a dispute.

> 2. Discerning is a learned skill that takes dedication and practice. Just like any other skill, the more disciplined you are, the more accurate you will become.

> 3. As a person's ability to discern increases, the matters that come before him or her become more complicated and carry greater consequences. Friends, colleagues, and clients begin to recognize the reliability of his or her opinion and come to them for help.

The story of King Solomon of Israel and his order to "split the baby" is an enduring example of great discerning that is often referred to by legal commentators on television talk-shows. It is found in the Old Testament in 1 Kings 3:16-28:

> Now two prostitutes came to the king and stood before him. One of them said, "My lord, this woman and I live in the same house. I had a baby while she was there with me. The third day after my child was born, this woman also had a baby. We were alone; there was no one in the house but the two of us. During the night this woman's son died because she lay on him. So she got up in the middle of the night and took my son from my side while I your servant was asleep. She put him by her breast and put her dead son by my breast. The next morning, I got up to nurse my son – and he was dead! But when I looked at him closely in the morning light,

I saw that it wasn't the son I had borne." The other woman said, "No! The living one is my son; the dead one is yours." But the first one insisted, "No! The dead one is yours; the living one is mine." And so they argued before the king. The king said, "This one says, 'My son is alive and your son is dead,' while that one says, 'No! Your son is dead and mine is alive.'" Then the king said, "Bring me a sword." So they brought a sword for the king. He then gave an order: "Cut the living child in two and give half to one and half to the other." The woman whose son was alive was filled with compassion for her son and said to the king, "Please, my lord, give her the living baby! Don't kill him!" But the other said, "Neither I nor you shall have him. Cut him in two!" Then the king gave his ruling: "Give the living baby to the first woman. Do not kill him; she is his mother." When all Israel heard the verdict the king had given, they held the king in awe, because they saw that he had wisdom from God to administer justice. (New International Version)

This situation required tremendous wisdom and discerning. The first woman's story describes such cruel behavior as to be unbelievable. Solomon had to wonder, "Could the second woman have been so selfish and cold-hearted that she might do such a thing? Yet, her accuser sounds believable." This would be quite a dilemma for anyone to unravel. But Solomon, having surely heard the cases of hardened liars before, knew what to do. He had to take the initiative to cause the truth to surface. And it worked. The second woman exposed her lack of love for the baby, making Solomon's decision obvious.

Anyone who has visited a prison, watched divorce court, or worked at a return desk in a retail store; knows how convincingly people can lie. A discerning person, who takes on the task of judging an issue, will want to be sure of the facts. But most importantly, we need to be certain that our cause is just—that we should be involved.

We should not take a position in an argument where we have no established authority to make a judgment, thus uselessly taking our time and focus away from our primary responsibilities.

Care About People

In a keeping the promise culture, we express our care for the customer by doing things right. And, we express our care for our colleagues through acts of kindness, encouragement, and support when things aren't going "right." We learn to care for one another through our own trials:

> When we have tried to work while family problems
> burden our ability to think;
> When we have endured loneliness and the heartbreak
> of broken relationships;
> When we have experienced the trauma of loss and
> failure;
> When we have faced unbearable pressures, and the
> agonies of waiting;
> Then we will know how to care for one another.

KEEPING
THE PROMISE

CHAPTER 5
EXPECT PERSONAL
RELIABILITY

☞ Promise

☞ ZD Attitude

☞ ZD Processes

☞ Vocational Values

☞ Personal Values

We further recognize that we must be honest and reliable people, at home and at work, and that we must share personal values that will allow us to trust and depend upon one another. Those values are Ethical Dependability and Personal Authenticity.

PART I – ETHICAL DEPENDABILITY:
A MEASURE OF OUR TRUSTWORTHINESS
IN PRACTICAL MATTERS

For nine years I traveled to St. Petersburg, Russia to oversee a humanitarian medical outreach to the poor and elderly. As a result, I became part of a special international effort called the Kissinger-Sobchak Commission which was organized to help solve the infrastructure problems of St. Petersburg and create ways to enable commerce. Our goal was to develop strategic initiatives that would simultaneously fulfill these objectives. As co-chair of the health care subcommittee, I was facilitating collaborations between government, business, and charitable entities, but when the Commission had general meetings, most of our time was spent discussing Russia's unethical business culture.

By the time I joined the Commission, we had completed three remodeling projects, organized specialized clinics for the elderly, and distributed several shipments of medicine throughout the city. Managing resources in Russia could be terrifying, so I was often asked by commission members and other westerners what our foundation was doing to overcome the "ethical nightmares" that doing business in the former Soviet Union presented. Our strategy was simple: We were diligently following sound business fundamentals. That meant we had to keep very accurate records of our activities and maintain precise communications with everyone who might affect our processes. Not only that, we had made the effort to learn their culture and spend time with them to build strong working relationships. But my secret weapon was a young man who blushed when he lied.

Remember the Voice of Influence

Sergei had been hired as one of my translators. He was just completing his Masters Degree in languages and had never had a regular job. However, his part-time experiences as a translator for foreign businessmen had piqued his interest in business. He was particularly attracted to our work because it combined all of the difficulties of operating an import-export business along with the charitable motives his Lithuanian grandmother had taught him during his long summer visits when he was a child. The concept of charity was considered anti-Soviet since the "state" was supposed to be everyone's benefactor. So to be taught such things was quite unusual in Russia, but not nearly as unusual as being taught "ethics."

Sergei's grandmother had done an excellent job. Not even the politically-correct Soviet brainwashing he had received at the University could make him reject "his grandmother's voice." When he was forced to recite the lies of the Soviet doctrine, he avoided conflict by lowering his head in shame. Or when someone told a lie in his presence, he would lower his head and blush. I routinely found myself in business meetings with Russians who had no ethical or moral restraint. When I would sense that what they were saying was less than reliable, I would catch a glimpse of Sergei's countenance. Those pink cheeks were like my own private lie detector.

I discovered this strategically vital trait on Sergei's second day on the job. He and his wife, who was also a part-time translator, were late for work. When I asked them why they were late, she produced a less-than-convincing story about having missed their train. It was then that I noticed Sergei's head lowered and his cheeks flushed. After I asked both of them a few revealing questions and provided some gentle correction, I met privately with him to discuss his goals. When I explained the kind of ethics and discipline I required, his face brightened. I soon discovered how closely I was resonating with "his grandmother's voice." As he shared the things she had taught him, there was immediate synergy between us. It was upon that basis, and knowing that I could easily train him in the essentials of business, that I promoted him to represent me in the most sensitive areas of my work. Over time, the reliability of our relationship was proven by Sergei's consistent trustworthiness in practical matters.

Every fundamentally ethical person can remember the influential voice of someone teaching them right from wrong. And just like my experiences with Sergei, when I teach business ethics or rally a business team to higher standards, I am depending upon my listeners being stirred to respond to that voice. Almost nothing that I have written in this book, speak about at a seminar, or counsel a business leader about ethics, is new information. It is only a renewal of what people have already known. Like many of my western colleagues trying to do business in Russia, I learned that no one can be truly successful without building upon a reliable foundation.

Acquire a Disciplined and Prudent Life

Who among us has not said, "I would like to do that all over again with what I now know." When we look back at how things "could have been," we can see how some of the most important decisions we have made were affected by our values. Greed, passion, or the personal need for power may have caused us to say "yes" to a risky plan when a more secure, disciplined person would have declined. Or careful and prudent analysis could have helped us properly evaluate the ethics of a business relationship that would later prove to be unsavory. There might also have been times when our fear of failure or questionable judgment neutralized us, and left us unable to take advantage of reasonable opportunities when they occurred.

We begin to shape our character early in life as we learn the principles that will become the foundation for our values and strategies. They include the significance of truth, what is just and fair, the difference between responsible and irresponsible actions, respect for the rights and property of others, the need for compassion and faithfulness in relationships, and how to exercise moral restraint. Everything else we learn or do is affected by these fundamentals.

A person's value system operates like a program in a computer. It is a complex set of interrelated ideas, learned experiences, and personal theories through which information is processed, analyzed, and output as actions to be taken. It includes all the values and strategies a person has collected over his or her lifetime along with the various priorities he or she has assigned them. When we have to make a decision, this program with all of its preset ideas and concepts (good and bad, accurate and inaccurate) begin to converge on the problem in an effort to come to a conclusion about the correct action to take and the strength with which it should be executed. Changing the viewpoint of just one item in our program from an unreliable to a reliable value can have enormously positive effects, especially when it brings sobering discipline to our thinking.

EXPECT PERSONAL RELIABILITY

The CEO culture sometimes questions a manager's "vision" if he or she does not press early and often for corporate growth. In other words, we are taunted to take presumptive action, without carefully developed plans, by people looking for quick results. Personally, I would much prefer that someone question my lack of vision before I succeed, than to have them question my wisdom after I have failed. To be sure that we are pursuing the right agenda, we should judge the validity of our vision by answering each of the following questions:

1. Do I have a sense of *intellectual integrity* about this idea? Are the thoughts and motives that are energizing me reliable? Are my plans really clear? Do my gifts and talents naturally support what I am considering?

2. Do I have a clear *moral conscience* about this plan? Am I at peace, and are the steps I have taken producing peace in me? Or, do I really feel uneasy, but have pushed on because I want or need something more than I should?

3. Am I being *faithful to the task*? Are my actions reasonable when I take steps to fulfill my objective, or do I find myself becoming unreasonably aggressive? Am I carefully stewarding my responsibilities or just forcing things to happen?

4. Am I making a *reasonable judgment*? Does my plan pass the test of common sense, or am I rationalizing facts and events? Am I really speaking truth to myself, or is there conflict in my heart?

These are difficult questions that deeply probe our values. But they must be answered to avoid the unnecessary consequences of an undisciplined decision.

Communicate with Intellectual Integrity

A person with intellectual integrity thinks and communicates with honesty and fairness. He or she presents opinions and evaluations honorably and with propriety, always trying to give an accurate representation of what he or she believes are the facts in any situation. He or she is guided by a sense of principle that is above self-interest and which is comfortable with even the most intense scrutiny. These are essential attributes in any person because the credibility of political, social, or economic debate; the soundness of democratic processes, and the reliability of relationships are in question when the intellectual integrity of a person is in doubt.

Breaches of intellectual integrity are emerging in all parts of our society. The honest representation of facts and figures is routinely being displaced by lying, deception, and various forms of manipulation. A war of perception, waged through what is tactically viable for the moment, not on what is fair, right, or true, dominates the media and the marketplace. In advertising, social actions, and political debates, the presenters are often depending on the listeners' ignorance of the biased methods they have used in their opinion polls. Or they may be relying on their ability to sway the listener with deliberately inaccurate rhetoric. The self-serving manipulation of words—or spin—has become an accepted professional skill. Although spin can produce the desired results in sales, memberships, contributions, and votes, its benefits are short-lived.

I worked with a client a few years ago who asked me to help him review the organizational design of his already quite profitable business. As we went through the preliminary training with his senior staff, we quickly discovered that there were serious differences of opinion about how the company's goals might be changed. This kind of conflict is not unusual since there is always some resistance associated with organizational change. We knew that we would have to discuss the ideas and viewpoints of everyone who would be affected until we reached agreement. It was important to patiently move toward the new vision. But as our training progressed, this particular situation became unusually combative.

One day during a coffee break, we were all sharing stories about week-end interests, when I realized what was wrong. Everyone in the room was much younger than the CEO and myself and had participated in what is commonly referred to as public education's "values clarification" programs. These programs were intended to make students free thinkers by teaching them to not allow anyone to impose values on them. While the CEO and I had both been educated in a public school environment which taught the importance of intellectual integrity, the others had been taught that integrity was a relative concept with no absolute borders. They had been trained to resist values-based accountability and thus had been intellectually and morally crippled, not able to unselfishly negotiate for the common good. This is one reason why so many people we encounter each day really do not believe that honesty and self-restraint are essential to a reasonable conversation.

Be Governed by Moral Conscience

Moral conscience is the power source for our moral behavior. It refers to much more than the chasteness or modesty of our sexual life and other private behaviors. It includes the concepts of self-restraint, the decent and humane treatment of others, respect for life and authority, principled and responsible policies, and all of those things which consider the common good as an outcome. It is broader than intellectual integrity. Moral conscience is the traffic director of our thought processes and moral behaviors. It gives us the strength to make difficult choices and stay the course in hard times.

The loss of our moral conscience as a nation has become very problematic. People have dramatically lowered their moral standards. Rape, sexual harassment, pedophilia, drug abuse, and fraud, along with other dangerous expressions of personal moral failures, have hit our country like an epidemic both at home and at work. One of the most pathetic and terrifying things to see is a person who has lost or is losing his or her conscience. In both my business and pastoral counseling, I have encountered several people who were so stunningly without conscience that they defied understanding. A businessman once came to my office to discuss what he called "personal problems." I occasionally had interviews with men whose friends had referred them to me for personal or spiritual counsel, so I expected it to be a routine first visit. But not long into our discussion, he very casually mentioned that he was facing legal charges for "touching" a little girl in his neighborhood. He said it in such a matter-of-fact manner that he might as well have been talking about a business loan. There was no sense of urgency or remorse about the man whatsoever and when I made a comment about the seriousness of the charges he looked me straight in the eye and said with a light chuckle, "I don't get it. I mean, what's all of the fuss about. She's only six years old. She doesn't even know what I did. There's really been no harm."

The pedophile who sat across from me in my office that day was dressed in a conservative business suit and looked like any middle-aged family man. He had a wife and children of his own and lived in a nice neighborhood where families thought they could trust one another. He went to work every day and even attended church, so there was no reason for his neighbors to have suspected what he was capable of doing, unless they had known about the video tapes he had stashed around his home, or his choice of websites. If they had followed him to work and witnessed the cool manipulation of his customers, they might have been alarmed. Or if they had called one of the business contacts he bragged about, they might have discovered, as his mortgage banker had, that his work history was not as impressive as he had often stated. But whenever he was caught in a misdeed, he would calmly lie and discredit his accuser. He was a special kind of predator called the "white-collar psychopath," (Hare, 1993) whose smooth, articulate demeanor allowed him to blend into almost any community undetected.

My first encounter with someone who demonstrated such an extreme lack of conscience had come years before when a friend asked me to help counsel a man from a prominent Christian family who had become a Satanist. For our entire session he boldly and defiantly described his participation in unspeakable rites and sacrifices, including murder. I was so shocked that I had trouble breathing. I have been asked many times how good people can end up in this kind of trouble. My answer is the same one that was whispered to me many years ago, "One step at a time." Just like a young man learning to smoke or to drink scotch, he had to have ignored and overcome the nauseating natural repulsions of his body and soul, and willed himself to continue. Although his story was heartbreaking and gruesome, it was a good lesson how each of us is capable of sinking deeper into personal depravity or crime.

Demonstrate Task Faithfulness

Personal responsibility is the hallmark of task faithfulness. A person who is task faithful can be depended upon. He is dutiful, constant, dedicated to his responsibilities, and unwavering in the fulfillment of his word. His stewardship is proven and he has the confidence of his superiors, peers, and subordinates. He is the one people turn to when they want things to work right, run on time, and be there when they are needed. He is devoted to his relationships and his family is carefully nurtured. His presence adds a level of certainty to any endeavor, and he carefully manages his time, energy, and resources. A faithful person generates faith and hope in those around him and brings a sense of security to his family and work.

Being faithful is so fundamental to a person's stewardship of authority and processes that when it is not proven, it is certain to create unwanted surprises. Faithful people can be taught the information, skills, and methods they will need to perform well. But building an organization upon even the most highly-educated and talented person whose faithfulness is in question, is a recipe for crisis. Every manager will face crunch-times when the commitments he or she has made are tested by the shortage of time, money, and energy. It is when we tackle these challenges that we discover the importance of faithfulness. When I think back through all the instances where I struggled to make a deadline and succeeded, it was faithful people who made the difference, not money or resources. It is during those pressurized events that human bonds are built and trustworthiness is proven. If we have noticed the signs of unfaithfulness in a person and have ignored or rationalized them away, we can be assured that we will pay the penalty when crunch-times come.

Many managers facing business failure discover that they had focused their energies only on those parts of their businesses they most enjoyed. They had either ignored other essential areas, or delegated them to people they later discovered to be unfaithful.

When a crisis developed, they would confess having had a nagging concern that they had not been paying enough attention to the areas from which the problems eventually arose. They would usually say things like: "I can't do everything and be everywhere," "Nobody's perfect," "I kept trying to find the time," or "I'm just not very good at that." These explanations may sound reasonable, but most of the time they are just cop-outs. They are unanswerable defenses which are intended to produce sympathy or deflect guilt. The truth is that we always find the ways and the means to do the things that are important to us. When we don't, there are usually specific reasons such as:

1. Personal or professional inexperience. One of the best ways to gain experience is to be faithful in another person's business. Apprenticing can provide insight and wisdom that education alone can't provide. It can be very enlightening to observe the processes and pressures of leading an organization without having to suffer the full consequences. It is a luxury which is often overlooked by young people who have ambitions and visions of their own. Those of us who didn't serve an apprenticeship, or who failed to pay attention when we did, have missed important opportunities to learn how to set priorities, test our motivations, and understand the consequences of neglected responsibilities. The things we experience as an apprentice can mature our attitudes and help us gain the advantage of being able to more correctly judge our own or another person's faithfulness.

2. Naive or undisciplined methods. While I was going to college, I worked at a car dealership. Working there was chaotic and there were all kinds of things that could go wrong to make a customer unhappy and spoil a deal. I learned quickly that unless I followed up on every phase of the sale,

financing, preparation, and delivery of a customer's car, the result could be an unsatisfied customer and the loss of a commission. It made me angry that other people's mistakes kept costing me money and that I had to do so much follow-up. It probably was unfair, but grumbling didn't change the circumstances. I finally stopped complaining about everyone else's failures and disciplined myself to regularly visit the finance office and service department to make sure that the things the customer had specifically asked for, as well as those that I knew he would expect, were completed properly and on time. Sometimes, I found that I had made errors in submitting paperwork. But even when I had done everything right, I learned how easily unintentional mistakes could be made by others. This required me to develop relationships in every part of the organization and helped me to gain a greater appreciation for what each person did in making my sale complete.

3. Priorities that are not properly balanced. Our work is usually so much a part of our life that we tend to spend the majority of our time and energy there. And rightly so, because being faithful to our work is an important measure of our faithfulness with our gifts and talents. But we can become so absorbed in our work that we forget its purpose—to support a family and our greater agenda for life. We all have to understand that the time we take away from our businesses to be with our families is time well spent. It is a true measure of our love for our family that we not only support them through our work, but that we nurture them with our time, energy, and wisdom.

4. The personal need to escape pressures. The pressures of a family or business can cause a person

to want to escape into something that is mentally or emotionally less demanding. It is interesting to me that a person who is facing work problems rarely escapes into family activities. It's usually golfing, fishing, shopping, or worse yet, another relationship. Alcoholism and drug addiction are very often the evidence of a person's attempts to escape the pressures and pains of life. When people are somehow shackled and unable to solve a problem, they tend to escape the frustration or fear of failure through some mind-numbing activity. People are generally uncomfortable facing their fears or vulnerabilities. They don't like to talk about them to their husbands, wives, friends, or others by seeking counsel because when they do decide to share with others and don't find immediate solutions, they feel even more insecure or weak. When a manager decides to hide his or her problems this way, it can have devastating effects on a business.

Use Reasonable Judgment

Reasonable judgment is the logical product of a person's wisdom and common sense. It supports the concepts of equity and justice in a civil society because a great part of our law hinges on the principle of what a reasonable person would say or do in a given situation. If someone is going to judge our work or make decisions that affect our personal life, we ideally want them to be diligent, logical, and analytical in the pursuit of facts. Then we expect them to be rational, prudent, and discerning in the analysis of those facts. As they sift through the options available to them, we hope that they will be consistent and sensible. And finally, we want their judgment to be wise, judicious, and fair. In short, what we are expecting is that they will deliberate faithfully, with intellectual integrity and moral conscience, in arriving at a reasonable judgment.

There is a Russian proverb which President Ronald Reagan made famous during the negotiation of the nuclear treaties with Russia. It is simply "trust, but verify." It means that two people can make an agreement that each trusts the other will fulfill. But to be sure, they should verify each other's actions. Sometimes people act offended when you verify their faithfulness. When you come back to check their work, count the money, or talk to a customer, they feel like it is an expression of your lack of trust in them. I have learned to explain to people that I can confidently verify their work because I do trust them, and I am sure that I will find faithfulness in the accounting or analysis. It is helpful to our working relationship for them to know that I trust them because I have verified so many times and found them to be faithful. And it is particularly important for both of us when I must give an account to others about the faithfulness of those under my authority. To a faithful person, accountability is not a threat, it is a friend. It is another opportunity to allow his or her faithfulness to shine through. In fact, checking the validity of a person's promise is the most basic expression of reasonable judgment.

Alexis DeTouqueville, in his landmark book, *Democracy in America*, recognized that the strength of America's democracy was related to its goodness and that its goodness was related to "mores" or moral conscience found in expressions of personal faith. He pointed out that if these important fibers in the fabric of public life were to deteriorate, that democracy itself would fail. Unfortunately, DeTouqueville accurately predicted the decline of ethics in America. Our concept of a civil society has deteriorated along with its loss of intellectual integrity and moral conscience. As a result, we can no longer depend upon our leaders to produce reasonable judgments.

I learned a great lesson in Russia about what happens to a civil society when their ability to make reasonable judgments degrades. Russia suffers from the effects of what I call a "moral holocaust." Intellectual integrity, moral conscience, and faithfulness in personal actions were systematically extinguished by the policies of the Soviet era. The moral and economic abuses of the Czars, coupled with their selfish misuse of Russia's resources, not only crippled the economy, but presented socialists with both the rationale and opportunity for revolution. The Leninist socialists intended to prevent such future social and economic indulgences as those which occurred under the Czars. To accomplish their goals, they secularized society, eliminated individual faith and responsibility, and replaced common sense social and moral values with sterile, illogical humanistic values. The result is a society that lacks the ability to make reasonable judgments and conduct business fairly.

PART II – PERSONAL AUTHENTICITY: A MEASURE OF OUR RESOLVE TO LIVE A CONSISTENT LIFE

During the past few years, there has been an increasingly intensive battle waged between the two main political parties in America about the inconsistencies they claim to have observed in one another's candidates. The Democrats are regularly trying to dig up inconsistencies in the lives of Republican candidates while the Republicans are busy doing the same for the Democrat's candidates. However, as I have listened to the often foolish nature of their arguments, I can't help but wonder whether the facts really matter to either side. They spend so much time and money tugging at our hearts and minds about things that often can't be proven that there is rarely a reasonable conversation about policies. Apparently, they would prefer to influence our perceptions without providing us with reliable facts. But one thing is certain: Both parties know that the perception of inconsistencies between a candidate's stated values and practiced values could negatively influence the voters.

Trying to discover personal inconsistencies has become a national pastime with print and news media, Internet websites, talk-shows, and various forms of "gotcha" journalism competing against one another for "the story." But the only reason they have a market for such things is that, if true, it matters to a large number of Americans. And for some of the characters in the various "morality plays," being able to turn the interests of the public toward another institution's inconsistency and away from their own is good business. So it is not unusual to have one perpetrator deliberately creating negative story-lines against another to compete for votes, market shares, and other things that translate into money and power.

With all of the tension and confusion that these tactics have created, people could be expected to turn to their faith to find relief. But sadly, many of our religious institutions have also become suspect. They are often just as involved in "spin" as the business or political sectors. For instance, I am sure the Roman Catholic Church has worked hard turning our attention away from the thousands of cases of priest-on-parishioner pedophilia which have plagued their institution virtually around the world for many decades. When you listen to the public rhetoric, the bishops often appear to be more interested in protecting their institution than cleaning up what has become an alarming pattern of behavior that seriously conflicts with their stated values.

The public's awareness of the inconsistencies in our political and religious institutions has grown dramatically over the past decade along with the threat of terrorism. In 1993, I received a private U.S. Government briefing about various Muslim extremist activities in the world. Of course, there had been the World Trade Center bombing, but I had no idea that there were literally dozens of armed conflicts around the world involving Muslim extremists. On virtually every continent there were and continue to be wildly irrational examples of Muslim faith in action. Most people thought the horrifying events of September 11, 2001 were the ultimate in perverted religious thinking, but we had not yet seen the televised beheadings which have now taken place around the world, not just in Iraq. For those of us who are not Muslims, and hopefully for the majority of those who are, there can be no rationale for such vile inconsistencies between their stated and practiced values.

Recognizing that there are millions of honest, well-intended congregants from every religion, apparently, none of our religious cultures have been exempt from gross inconsistencies and, at times, unexplainable scandal. I read an article written by a group of evangelical Christians which said that at least a third of the men participating in their so-called revival movement had admitted to having on-going "problems" with pornography. That's not surprising when you think of all the moral and financial scandals that were exemplified by the televangelists. Notwithstanding the huge differences between their stated and practiced values, they still insist on their self-proclaimed status as the leaders of the "moral majority." Meanwhile, millions of discouraged believers are leaving the mainline churches around the world, confirming that there are a lot more than just "problems" with many other issues. Maybe it's time for our religious, political, and business leaders to rethink the goals and objectives of their institutions and participate a little more realistically in fulfilling the promises they have made.

Our leaders are causing us to spend far too much time wallowing in the mire of someone else's contribution to our unethical culture while far too little is being done to renew the values that will change it. When our religious, political, and business institutions all begin to lose the trust of the people they serve, the slide down the proverbial slippery slope has begun. The only thing that can effectively reverse this trend is a grass-roots movement "of the people." In a free-market democracy, the customer's requirements will always prevail. We just need a few more reasonably concerned customers insisting on a renewal of ethics in America.

Embrace the Obligations of Leadership

The subject of leadership has been written and argued about for centuries with various theories on how to identify, measure, and reproduce it. But leadership is clearly indicated by what we do when the weight of responsibility settles across our shoulders and we understand for the first time that life has the potential of being more than we can handle. Only a casual review of the ethical standards in America is required to see how far we have declined. Sometimes what we see and hear in a single day can be overwhelming, but we have not yet gone so far we can't recover. A "turn-around" could begin and be carried forward by individuals who decisively step forward as agents for change.

Our objective is not, should not be, and can never be, to become a culture of whistleblowers or ethical fanatics, but to build a social and business culture with people who are intent on keeping the promises they make. To do so, you must only believe that you can make a difference and then take responsibility to change the places where you live and work. I always tell people when I am consulting on organizational issues that our goal is not to change the world, or even the industry in which they work, only their company. However, if one or two leaders in an industry successfully change their culture, the others must follow to stay competitive. In the meantime, keep focused on what you can do today to excite people about both the need for change and the potential benefits of a *keeping the promise* culture.

You can't expect unethical or immoral people to feel comfortable with the idea of a keeping the promise culture, because it will limit their ability to build the coalitions they need to succeed in their predatory behaviors. So expect some opposition and consider it an honor to be challenged. There will also be those who will be uncomfortable enforcing the kind of accountability required in a keeping the promise culture. I have talked to people who are so averse to confronting ethical issues that they would rather be labeled as a *coward* than be known as a *snitch*. A snitch is the name self-indulgent people use to describe someone who has been unsuccessful in holding them personally accountable and then reports their immoral, unethical, or criminal behavior to the proper authorities. Managers are now called snitches when they report behaviors that are inconsistent with fulfilling the promises they have made to their customers and shareholders. However, it is a manager's duty to the customer and to his hard-working colleagues to challenge anyone whose behaviors will impede their progress toward the promise. When managers and other leaders step forward, we should openly support their efforts.

Be Diligent in the Use of Your Faith

One of the dictionary definitions of *faith* is: fidelity (or faithfulness) to one's promises; something that is believed with strong conviction as a system of religious beliefs. A classical Greek definition of faith is: to be morally persuaded of the truth. The success we experience as managers and ethical change-agents will depend greatly upon how morally persuaded we become about the need for change, and then how faithfully we model the values and principles of our management doctrine. But the most emotionally challenging test for managers is to live consistently with those things that we are morally persuaded are true and right, when the decisions we make will affect people's motivations or livelihood.

As managers, we are obligated to empower the promise by keeping the fire of the ZD heart attitude burning brightly. An essential element for "fanning the flame" is getting it right on the decisions we make. But the more important question is: How can we know our information is reliable? Simply put, reliable methods produce reliable results. The method I have learned to rely upon and which has repeatedly proven its dependability at home and at work is called the "scientific method." All the activities of the scientific method are characterized by an attitude that stresses "rational impartiality" or the unbiased search for reliable facts and truth. Although this method of inquiry involves some detailed techniques for investigation and analysis, my intention is to emphasize only its basic tenets, which are very user-friendly. Following are the steps of the scientific method:

1. *Observation.* When we become aware of a specific problem, circumstance, event, question of fact or phenomenon that requires an explanation, the first step is to gather enough information by simple observation or inquiry to clearly state the problem and its significance.

2. *Hypothesis.* On the basis of the initial information that is acquired, a hypothesis (or general idea) is formed about what the information means or how it explains an unknown or unproven issue.

3. *Investigation.* The implications of the hypothesis (the facts that you think can be proven to be true) are then further considered and tested by additional observations, investigations, and, when possible, experiments.

4. *Testing.* If the investigation produces additional facts that are in disagreement with the original hypothesis or its implications, the hypothesis is modified or discarded in favor of a new hypothesis, which is then subjected to further investigation and tests. This process is repeated until the results of investigating and testing a hypothesis and its implications are all in agreement and can be easily repeated by another investigator.

5. *Conclusion.* When a hypothesis and its implications are consistently proven to be accurate by each aspect

of investigation and testing, they are considered to be reliable.

Diligently using the scientific method to research the facts until we are morally persuaded of the truth does three very important things: First, it proves whether or not we have the truth. Second, it is a discipline that builds patience and self-restraint into our character. And third, it provides opportunities for people to learn about the authenticity of our leadership style.

Work to Keep a Clear Conscience

The kind of cold, heartless arguments against truth that at one time were the private venue of hardened criminals are now routinely heard in our homes, schools, businesses, and yes, our churches, synagogues, and mosques. While young and old alike argue for their right to exhibit selfish, vulgar, unethical, and insensitive behaviors, "Don't judge me" has become the standard defense for a worldwide culture that rejects defining right and wrong. The blush of embarrassment is now rarely observed. We are living in an era where people from every walk of life have learned to ignore the facts and switch the rules when it suits them and to rehearse their lies until they show "no-conscience."

My consulting work has regularly thrust me into situations where I must console managers who are stupefied by the range of misbehavior they have discovered about who they thought were "normal" people. When I was in Russia, I saw so many behaviors I could barely have imagined by normal people that I coined this simple phrase: What I get away with today, becomes tomorrow's law. In other words, when our bad behaviors go unchallenged, we begin to rationalize them so that our conscience is no longer bothered. With enough repetitions, we can actually convince ourselves that bad things are normal, and if not legal, then at least they shouldn't be illegal.

I have learned two important lessons from observing these things: First, I want to always be diligent to keep a clear conscience myself. To do that, I must be willing to admit and correct my mistakes as I become aware of them. Second, as a manager, if I allow someone's bad behaviors to go unchallenged, I am allowing them to move—one step at a time—toward increasingly bad behaviors. Eventually, I will be faced with a much more difficult task or even tragedy. In the meantime, I might also be allowing someone to poison the keeping the promise culture. I decided that if I failed to act properly to correct bad behavior, that I was being unfaithful to the poorly-behaving person, his or her coworkers, and especially the customer.

Like any process, our conscience is growing either clearer or duller day-by-day as we take simple steps that are honest and ethical or steps that are dishonest and unethical. To illustrate this, imagine a "clear conscience continuum," with good behaviors going from the center of the continuum out to infinity on the left and bad behaviors to the right. When I explain this in a classroom, I ask the participants some questions to help give perspective to the continuum. Strangely, the answers are always the same: 1. Who is the nicest person you can imagine, someone whose good deeds exemplify a clear conscience? Answer: Mother Theresa. 2. Who is the meanest, nastiest, most cruel person you can imagine, someone whose bad deeds exhibit no conscience? Answer: Hitler. 3. Is there anyone better than Mother Theresa? Answer: God. 4. Is there anyone worse than Hitler? Answer: Satan. So they are now looking at a continuum that looks something like this:

Clear Conscience Continuum

God ← M.Theresa ←← ←← →→ →→ →→ → Satan
Good Behavior   Bad Behavior
Hitler

I continue the questioning. 5. O.K. then, where is your place on this continuum? Answer: Blank stares. 6. I would expect most normal people to be somewhere between Mother Theresa and Hitler, wouldn't you agree; but where? Answer: A sudden chorus of "Yes" followed by more blank stares. 7. Let's try another one. Where is your boss on this continuum? Answer: Laughter mixed in with a lot of people yelling, "Satan."

The truth is that we cannot know where we are on the clear conscience continuum, except to compare our own behaviors with that of someone else. I know that I am better behaved than Hitler, while I am obviously not as good as Mother Theresa. So even if I know that much, I still don't know where I am, or where you are, unless I compare our behaviors against a known standard. I can, however, know whether I am moving toward Mother Theresa or Hitler by the individual choices I make each day. I can also make the same judgment about another person by observing the pattern of behaviors in his or her life. As a manager, I am well within my authority and responsibility to be aware of such things, first in my own life, and then in the behaviors of my staff and colleagues, especially if I have reliable facts.

Subject Yourself to Reality Checks

A common technique in human services work is to help people face the reality of their behaviors. Criminals, addicts, the mentally ill, the behaviorally challenged, and even normal people doing bad things must be able to discover and accept a realistic perspective about themselves before they will be able to keep themselves turned toward the good side of the clear conscience continuum. This is a particularly difficult objective to achieve when a person has become entangled in addictive behavior, because their lack of reliable perspective about themselves often leads them into more serious addictions and criminal behavior instead of back to reality. To complicate matters, sometimes people feel wrongly entitled to continue their destructive behavior, allowing others to unfairly bear the consequences.

One afternoon I received an urgent call from a family asking me to visit their son who had just been arrested. I didn't ask why, but assumed it was on another drug charge. When I arrived at the jail, the chaplain, who escorted me to the young man's cell, spoke to me in a fatherly tone and said, "Remember where you are and what you're doing. Keep alert. If you need help, just wave to the guard." It was a rather ominous instruction for a visit with a young drug addict. But as soon as I sat down, I realized why. The young man began sobbing and cried out, "I did it! I did it! I'm so sorry; I don't know what came over me." He then described in excruciating detail how, only hours before, he had murdered an innocent storekeeper who had refused to give him money so that he could buy drugs. It was a despicable and bloody crime and an act of senseless rage. But as unbelievable as it sounded, almost any addict could relate to the reservoir of anger that had accumulated within this young man, if not the crime itself. The habit that had started out years before with marijuana had become a consuming heroin addiction, creating the potential for any act that would satisfy his craving.

My next visit was even more startling. I found quite a different young man this time. If I had not already heard his horrific confession, he would have sounded completely believable when he said, "I'm innocent, you know. My parents have hired a good lawyer and he says we can beat the charge." After spending time with his lawyer, he was intent on speaking the legal language of the courtroom. Apparently, he had decided to rely upon his proven ability to manipulate his parents with lies. Before he was finished with them, they had spent all of their savings, re-mortgaged their home, and even asked me to be a character witness at his trial. I was so saddened by their plight that I only said this, "Tell your son I will be very happy to tell the truth and the whole truth, but he might prefer that I invoke my right to pastoral confidentiality and remain silent. Let it be his choice." Instead of clearing his conscience, pleading guilty, and probably getting a lighter sentence, he ended up on death row.

As managers, we often find ourselves helping someone separate truth and reality from their delusions. If we don't, they may continue to move the wrong way on the clear conscience continuum, causing our own career or business to unfairly end up on death row. It is imperative that we maintain reliable relationships with colleagues and fellow managers to help provide the "reality check" we need before we make a difficult management decision. This is especially the case when your decision involves someone with entitlement or addictive attitudes. And by the way, don't forget your C.E.N. Journal.

Let Your Life Be Your Message

One of the most imposing obstacles to people becoming more reliable in the work place is the inconsistent behaviors of those who teach and lead. For far too many people, their "message" is all they have. When you get closer and can see the pattern of behaviors in their home or work life, you may not be as enthusiastic about depending upon their reliability. Not that perfection should be required of anyone, but when the preacher is a pedophile, the school teacher is a Satanist, the nurse is an addict, the cop is a psychopath, or the CEO is a thief, it matters.

Imagine that you are the customer of any one of these people and that you became aware of the inconsistencies between their stated and practiced values. Your confidence in them would likely be diminished because there are risks associated with their inconsistent behaviors. If the preacher is a pedophile, which member of your family are you willing to subject to his counsel or leadership? If the nurse is an addict, which one of your family members are you willing to risk to his or her judgment in an intensive care unit? If the CEO is a thief, she is probably a liar too. Could you trust her enough to buy a house or car from her, or transact anything of importance? Could you work for her? How much risk to your career, livelihood, and family's well-being do these kinds of people represent? That's the kind of thing you should be considering, whether you are their customer or colleague and you know about their inconsistencies. When you want things to work right, run on time, or be there when you need them, these things matter. A person's authenticity or lack of it can have a dramatic effect on keeping the promise.

I learned a great lesson about how important personal authenticity can be to all the parties of a transaction when I was administering a hospital project in St. Petersburg, Russia. My personal staff consisted of two translators, an office assistant, the Russian equivalent of a C.P.A., and a deputy administrator. There was a lot of paperwork and I was increasingly involved in activities that required either document translation or interpreters. So the staff had decided they would like to hire a file clerk to free them up for more important things.

One morning, as the staff gathered in my office to organize the day's activities I noticed a new face sitting next to one of our translators. Her name was Natalya and, unknown to me, she was the unanimous choice of the staff to become the new clerk. She looked so young, that I could not have guessed she was there for an interview, thinking instead that she might be someone's younger sister or daughter. My staff was bilingual and we spoke English during these meetings, with the translators occasionally filling in the gaps. So Natalya, who could not speak English, sat quietly through the meeting smiling awkwardly as we bantered back and forth. As we finished, one of the assistants mentioned that Natalya was looking for work and asked me to speak with her following the meeting.

To be honest, I was facing a busy schedule and what would normally have been a courtesy I could happily extend, felt more like a burden to bear. But I dutifully agreed and began the interview by asking several questions through the translator. Natalya had a child-like countenance and a quiet personality although she had intelligent-looking eyes. I quickly discovered that she was nineteen, had no previous experience, except as a farm-laborer, and had not completed high school. She lived outside the city and had taken an hour-long train ride for the interview which ended politely and, I thought, unproductively. After the interview, the translator stayed behind and was soon joined by the rest of the staff to lobby on behalf of Natalya. They told me how she had endured an abusive childhood and had to overcome huge obstacles every day of her life, even to attend the meeting with me. The bottom line: They were all willing to help train her, if necessary on their own time, and most importantly, they were willing to guarantee her integrity and authenticity. It was a guarantee they had earned the right to make, so "little Natalya" was hired and started work that very day. The nickname "little Natalya" stuck because it distinguished her from our chief accountant who was also named Natalya.

She was never late, absent, or found idle. She worked joyfully and would do absolutely anything to help, including cleaning the office or running errands in the cold Russian winter. In just a few weeks she had reorganized our files and documents and was busy learning how to do simple entries for the bookkeeper. She also began answering the phone and transferring calls in both Russian and English. When we received medical shipments she might just as likely be found in the back of the truck unloading boxes or helping the doctors sort and classify the medicines. She also helped the professors organize their classrooms in our training center and made sure they had the supplies they needed for the English and word-processing classes. Every time someone discussed little Natalya, they would inevitably say, "She is very smart, and such a nice girl."

After about six months little Natalya asked me if she could begin taking English and computer classes. We had organized the classes so that our doctors and administrators could more effectively exchange information with the west and there was a long waiting list of professionals who wanted to participate. But who could resist little Natalya. The professors were amazed at her progress and in just a few months she was clicking away at her own keyboard, at her own desk in the chief accountant's office. You see, not only was little Natalya an authentic person, she was an authentic genius. And the authenticity of the relationships I had with my staff was the only reason she was given a chance. They saw her potential; they brought me the opportunity, and I nearly missed it. Except for the authenticity and reliability I attributed to my staff's guarantee, and our resolve to live a consistent life in a keeping the promise culture, little-Natalya might still be held tightly in the grip of abuse and we would have missed one of the great opportunities of a lifetime.

KEEPING THE PROMISE

CHAPTER 6
EMPLOY THE PROMISE

☞ Promise

☞ ZD Attitude

☞ ZD Processes

☞ Vocational Values

☞ Personal Values

☞ Mutual Respect, Accountability, Professionalism

Finally, we realize that a keeping the promise culture is built upon a foundation of mutual respect, accountability, and professionalism.

To employ means to *put to work*. So to employ the promise, you must begin to model the foundational values of a keeping the promise culture: mutual respect, accountability, and professionalism. First, renew these values in your own life and then share them in the workplace. As opportunities arise, widen the discussion to the specifics of vocational excellence and personal reliability. Whether you are the CEO of your company or just someone diligently laboring to overcome the ethical decline, you can help begin a renewal of the work ethic.

Mutual Respect: Treat People the Way You Want to Be Treated

One of the first things I observe when I visit a new client is whether or not people treat one another with respect. It is an important measure of the overall business environment because the license for bad behavior starts at the top of the organization. If people act in unrestrained ways, it is because they feel entitled to indulge themselves. It may mean that they are reacting to poor leadership traits such as tyranny or greed; or they may be acting badly because of the leader's general lack of interest in them. But when the employees treat one another with respect, it usually means their leader is modeling the right values and is treating people the way he or she would want to be treated.

I like to tour the facilities with the CEO so that I can see how people react to his or her presence. If they are quietly respectful, yet remain busy and focused, it indicates that the manager's presence is a normal experience for the staff. But if they are "over-the-top" and pull away from their work to gushingly greet the manager, it probably means that he or she is not often seen "where the work is done." CEOs who misinterpret the adoring praise of a rarely-seen staff as an indicator of a good attitude toward their leadership are usually surprised to learn that as soon as they return to the security of the administrative suite, the staff will return to a more cynical work ethic. In fact, a rare visit by a leader who is only feigning his or her interest can be easily discerned by the staff and can sometimes become a stimulant to bad behavior.

Mutual respect is demonstrated by much more than courteous, polite, and respectful behavior. It is also indicated by the way we share information with people who have a "need to know." When we make an important decision, the people most affected by that decision should be fully informed before they have an opportunity to hear a modified version of the truth through the "grapevine." The grapevine is the fastest moving and most destructive force to a business environment because it conveys incomplete facts and perceptions about what are often highly-charged topics. When people have been given less information than they need, they tend to create their own versions of the facts, often bringing unintended harm to people and processes. That's why confidentiality is not just a legal matter.

I was conducting some routine organizational research for a client when a mid-level manager approached me with a request to speak "confidentially." In just a few minutes she outlined the emotional abuse and harassment she and others had endured from their immediate superior, and that he had been able to deflect previous attempts to hold him accountable by threatening retaliation. The accusations were quite serious and the accuser was completely believable. However, the accused had always been able to portray himself as the victim of false accusations by carefully manipulating the company's very active grapevine.

I explained to the young woman that the only way to end the man's tyranny, if it could be proven, was to completely eliminate the grapevine from access to the investigation. That meant absolute confidentiality. She could share nothing of our discussion with anyone, not even the fellow sufferers she had named. I knew from experience that it was possible the accused could prove to be innocent, even though the initial facts were damning. Both he and his accuser had to be treated the way I would want to be treated, so that neither of them was unduly harmed.

The young woman kept her promise, as did the others I interviewed, until there was a complete picture and an irrefutably clear pattern of the accused man's behaviors. Weeks later, following the man's dismissal, each of the accusers recalled how they thought there was no investigation because of the lack of "buzz" on the grapevine and the sometimes increasingly-bad behavior of their superior. But they had kept their promises of confidentiality, as did the CEO who was sincerely concerned for their well-being, and they finally experienced justice.

Accountability: Upgrade from Loyal to Faithful

Loyalty is often referred to as an essential attribute in individual relationships and corporate human relations. But it falls short of the concept of "faithfulness" because loyalty too often requires us to restrain ourselves from discussing the truth. To be faithful, we must be unwavering in our commitments, always keep our promises, and never allow anyone to harm the person we serve, just as loyalty requires. But faithful people also have no fear of speaking the truth, especially to the one we serve. When someone expects us to obey without question, they are asking us to silence our conscience when we see and hear things that are wrong. This is the foundation for tyranny. Even in the military, loyalty is conditioned upon a clear conscience. No one is expected to obey an immoral or illegal order.

The concept of simple loyalty is dramatically lacking, especially in the context of the ethical decline in America. The most loyal people are members of organized crime, or are engaged in corporate fraud or political intrigue, exchanging their talents and energy for the short-term gains of power and money. But these often fiercely loyal people are moving the wrong way—one step at a time—on the clear conscience continuum. I have visited with several "loyalists" who ended up in prison, and they consistently tell me they could not have imagined when they started their own ethical decline what they would become capable of doing. In organized crime, the loyal man becomes a "made-man" by murdering someone, not just because he is ordered to kill, but to satisfy his needs for security, identity, and belonging. So why should we be surprised at the rise of unethical behavior by our growing culture of corporate loyalists?

Managers who demand loyalty instead of faithfulness may be admitting their inability to build influence with their staff through personal consistency, or worse, their unwillingness to be held accountable for their behaviors. Without compromising the positional authority they gain from the organizational chart, managers must be willing to subject their ideas to the scrutiny of their colleagues and subordinates. The hearts and minds of any corporate team should be won with vision, consistency, and the reasonable use of authority, not coerced by a demand for loyalty. The openness and collegiality of what is known in QM as the "quality circle" is an example of this more effective use of authority because it causes us to recognize one another's strengths and weaknesses and find the best solutions. This "circular authority" enables managers who are personally secure and vocationally certain to blend the authority gained vertically from the organization and laterally from personal influence into a dynamic, problem-solving synergy.

The human attribute that makes this form of leadership most effective is humility, which is best expressed by the willingness to be known for who we are. This is a rare commodity in today's supercharged corporate world. But when the humility of a leader connects with the values and principles of a keeping the promise culture, the results are predictably positive. People will be faithful and speak the truth.

Professionalism: Set a Clear
Standard for Doing Things Right

When the value of our work is clearly linked to fulfilling our customer's requirements, people will perform even the most mundane responsibilities with a Zero Defects attitude. So the key to maintaining a clear standard for doing things right is to never lose sight of the customer's needs. When we remind ourselves that the customer considers our promise to be a precious asset, it is much easier to answer the question: "How many defects are too many?" And when we empathize with the customer's experience, we can enthusiastically accept the challenge of professionalism: to give every fact, event, issue, or problem the diligence it is due, with a Zero Defects attitude.

As any sports coach will tell you, greatness is not found in the grand strategies, but in the disciplined execution of the fundamentals. The great athletes, artists, musicians, scientists, lawyers, architects, and so on, have at least one thing in common: They have all mastered the fundamentals of their vocation. This qualifies them to compete at a higher level with all the other professionals who have mastered the same fundamentals. Watching someone perform at a high professional level can be very moving. It causes us to think, and dream and set higher goals. So if you believe your calling is to be a professional manager, it should be very encouraging to discover that the great managers like W. Edwards Deming and Philip Crosby built their careers on the mastery of simple fundamentals. But if you just want to be the very best you can be in your chosen vocation, a professional who makes a difference, then the ethical decline in America is presenting you with an opportunity to shine.

To learn more about developing a Keeping the Promise™ culture *and* earn continuing education credits in ethics or management, register to attend our Business and Continuing Education Seminars. Contact Creative Management Services, Inc. at:

http://www.LarryKennedy.com
Email: Seminars@LarryKennedy.com